SAN FRANCISCO
49ERS
Where Have You Gone?

MATT MAIOCCO

www.SportsPublishingLLC.com

ISBN: 1-58261-994-8

Interior photos courtesy of the San Francisco 49ers, unless otherwise noted.

Publishers: Peter L. Bannon and Joseph J. Bannon Sr.
Senior managing editor: Susan M. Moyer
Acquisitions editor: Bob Snodgrass
Developmental editor: Regina D. Sabbia
Art director: K. Jeffrey Higgerson
Dust jacket design: Kenneth J. O'Brien
Project manager: Greg Hickman
Imaging: Heidi Norsen
Photo editor: Erin Linden-Levy
Vice president of sales and marketing: Kevin King
Media and promotions managers: Kelley Brown (regional),
      Randy Fouts (national), Maurey Williamson (print)

Printed in the United States of America

Sports Publishing L.L.C.
804 North Neil Street
Champaign, IL 61820

Phone: 1-877-424-2665
Fax: 217-363-2073
www.SportsPublishingLLC.com

To Sarah, Jane and Lucy

CONTENTS

PREFACE

Joe Thomas was the 49ers' general manager for two seasons in the late 1970s. But in that time he managed to do lasting harm to the organization—far worse than anything that shows up in the standings.

Thomas wanted to remake the 49ers in his own image. Therefore, he decided to do away with the past. Old photos, programs and memorabilia were tossed into a dumpster behind the team's Redwood City practice facility.

The past was ordered to be forgotten.

While the organization briefly turned its back on all former 49ers, anybody who watched the team during the 1950s, 1960s and 1970s could not—and would not—erase those memories.

One of those fans of the 49ers during the early years was George Seifert, who as a high-school student served as an usher for games at Kezar Stadium during the 1956 and 1957 seasons.

"My job was to point people to their seats, but it was basically just a way to get to watch the 49ers for free," he said.

And when he was not "working" the games, he found other inventive ways to watch the 49ers. Seifert was on the roof of a classmate's house on Frederick Street, adjacent to Kezar, when R.C. Owens made his first "Alley-Oop" catch in 1957.

Seifert's first love was the 49ers. He lived and died with the team—and with some of the organization's unpopular decisions. Seifert always had a sense of perspective and appreciation for the past during his eight-year run as head coach of the 49ers from 1989 to 1996.

"I remember how frustrated I was as a young man when 'Red' Hickey traded Y.A. Tittle to the New York Giants. 'How could that idiot coach do something like that?'" Seifert said. "Then I was the 'idiot coach' involved in trading Joe Montana. I thought of all the kids and what they had to be thinking of me."

San Francisco 49ers: Where Have You Gone? is a book intended to catch up with some of the interesting individuals throughout the team's history. After all, the rich tradition of the 49ers goes back much further than 1979, when head coach Bill Walsh took over as the central figure of the organization after owner Eddie DeBartolo fired Thomas.

In the process of writing these profiles, I tried to hit on many of the important games, moments and personalities that reflect the history of the organization. After all, it is a history that should be kept alive, not thrown into a dumpster.

The 49ers underwent an extreme makeover after the club bumbled to a league-worst 2-14 record in 2004. Owner John York hired Mike Nolan to be the 49ers' 15th head coach. York said one of the reasons he tabbed Nolan as his coach was because Nolan "understands what it means to be head coach of the San Francisco 49ers."

Nolan should know what it means. His father, Dick, was the 49ers' sixth head coach. He led the 49ers to the playoffs three times, including back-to-back trips to the NFC Championship Game in 1970 and 1971.

At Nolan's introductory press conference in January 2005 at a posh Nob Hill hotel, some of his father's former players were in attendance. The 49ers had taken another step to reconnect with the past.

Seifert said knowing the history of the 49ers helped him carry out his job, during which time he compiled a remarkable 108-35 record, including two Super Bowl titles.

"Even though I was considered a defensive coach, I wanted to make sure we always had an exciting offense," Seifert said. "The identity of the franchise from the early years had always been on offense."

Nolan echoed those comments upon accepting the job.

"A team needs to not only have its own identity," Nolan said, "but the identity of the city and the fans. I believe the winning tradition will carry on."

Seifert, who enjoys the retired life with homes in Bodega Bay and the Tahoe area, is still a fan of the football club he grew up following. And he said he is optimistic for the team's future because Nolan is no outsider.

"He has a deep-rooted sense of history about the team," Seifert said. "I think that background with the 49ers helps. There's an added juice to it. It helped me, and I'm sure it'll help him, too."

ACKNOWLEDGMENTS

During the course of researching and writing this book, I placed hundreds of phone calls in hopes of tracking down former San Francisco 49ers players from all eras. I was quite pleased with how well this project was received, as only a handful of individuals declined my interview requests.

Fittingly, there are 49 profiles in this book. Some of the players are all-time greats, and some are relatively obscure, but each serves a valuable purpose in the telling of the 49ers' history. I am especially appreciative of the individuals who shared their deeply personal stories and answered all my questions: David Kopay, Eason Ramson, Dan Audick, Keith Fahnhorst, Jeff Fuller and Delvin Williams, in particular. Audick also deserves a big assist for volunteering use of all his personal photos from recent 49ers Alumni Days.

I am grateful to my good friend R.C. Owens, who assisted me in getting in contact with many of the interview subjects for this book. "Alley-Oop" is probably the person most responsible for keeping the history of the 49ers alive through his efforts as the team's alumni coordinator for more than two decades.

Thanks to Keena Turner and Guy McIntyre for their assistance during the 49ers' Alumni Weekend in October of 2004. I am also appreciative to 49ers' human resource director Annette Snyder and benefits coordinator Sandy Fontana for their help. Bill Walsh was gracious with his time, as I interviewed him about many of the subjects I profiled for this book.

The 49ers public-relations staff was generous in allowing me to rummage through their files. Many thanks to the irreplaceable Kirk Reynolds and his wife, Teri, who set a great example of how to deal with adversity head-on during the tumultuous 2005 offseason. Good luck to them on their future endeavors. The first-rate staff Reynolds assembled was also helpful: Jason Jenkins, Fitz Ollison, Kristina Hartman, Kristin Johnson, Ryan Moore, Matt Kramer and Cindy Krawczyk. I'll miss working with Johnson, Moore and Kramer, who have moved onto other opportunities. Also, thanks to Tom Hastings, the team's manager of internet services.

This book would not have been complete without the photos of team photographer Michael Zagaris. Also, thanks to Brad Mangin, one of the most talented shooters in the business, for lending some of his work to the project.

Special thanks to *Oakland Tribune* columnist Carl Steward for sending me a copy of the legendary and thoroughly hysterical locker room exchange that took place between Monty Stickles and then-San Francisco Giants manager Frank Robinson. Alameda Newspaper Group sports editor Jon Becker was also helpful during this project.

Team historian Donn Sinn was helpful in my efforts to research this book. Also, thanks to the people in the newspaper room at the Oakland Main Library, who kicked me out only once for hording the microfiche machine. I thoroughly enjoyed reading the countless newspaper stories through the years that chronicled the men I profiled in this book. Thanks to Bob Snodgrass and the folks at Sports Publishing for asking me to do another book, and for developmental editor Gina Sabbia's commitment to the project.

Thanks to my dear friend Granville DeMerritt for trusting me with his original game programs from the 1948 and 1953 seasons. And, finally, a big assist goes to self-described 49ers FAN-atic Ron Lent, whose expertise and guidance I leaned upon from this project's inception. Ron answered numerous questions, served as an editor and offered helpful suggestions every step of the way.

VISCO GRGICH

Visco Grgich is an original in more ways than one. He was on the first 49ers team in 1946, where he distinguished himself as an original, period.

More than 50 years after his playing career ended with torn knee ligaments, and nearly 20 years since spending a couple weeks in the hospital after suffering a stroke, Grgich showed the same fire that made him one of the 49ers' first stars when the subject turned to his career.

While attending a 49ers alumni function, in October 2004, Grgich recounted his run-ins with the late Norm Van Brocklin, the Hall of Fame quarterback of the Los Angeles Rams. Grgich gave an animated description of the on-field tussle and the pledge right there in the middle of the game to meet in the Kezar Stadium tunnel after the game to settle the score.

Grgich, still boiling from emotions of the game, showed up at the agreed-upon spot afterward. Finally, Van Brocklin met him. He was decked out in a nice suit. Grgich was ready to rumble, but Van Brocklin diffused the situation. "You wanna grab a beer?" Van Brocklin asked.

Former teammate Bill "Tiger" Johnson said Grgich did not look like a football player when he wasn't wearing his football uniform. But on the field, Grgich was a terror.

"I especially remember the great days he had against Van Brocklin," Johnson said. "Every time we played the Rams, he would gobble up Van Brocklin. That was one guy Van Brocklin didn't want to see, and he'd get so angry at Visco."

Van Brocklin also handled the punting chores for the Rams. In 1951, Leo Nomellini and Grgich broke through the Rams line to block Van Brocklin's punt. Grgich went after Van Brocklin while Nomellini went after the ball. With Grgich blocking Van Brocklin, Nomellini scored the touchdown in a 44-17 rout over the Rams.

Grgich spent most of his adult life as a popular teacher and coach in the central California town of Oakdale, where he was always quick with an anecdote from his playing days with the 49ers.

The Yugoslavian-born Grgich moved to Seattle with his parents when he was in grade school, and eventually became known as "Swivel Hips Grgich," because he was the most elusive tailback in town. But his best route to professional football was on defense as a 5-foot-11, 220-pound nose guard.

VISCO GRGICH

Nose guard · Santa Clara · Ht. 5-11; Wt. 217
Born: January 19, 1923 · 49ers career: 1946-1952

Career highlights: Played on first 49ers team in 1946 ·
Named first-team All-AAFC in 1949 · Chosen to Pro Bowl in
1950, the first season the 49ers were in the NFL ·
Honorable mention All-NFL in 1950, 1952 · Wore
numbers 34, 38, 47 and 64 with 49ers.

Grgich was a charter member of the 49ers, turning down a scholarship to Notre Dame after playing for St. Mary's Pre-Flight. He signed a three-year, no-cut contract with the 49ers of the fledgling All-America Football Conference.

When the 49ers moved to the National Football League in 1950, he joined quarterback Frankie Albert, tackle Leo Nomellini, fullback Norm Standlee, and halfback John Strzykalski as the first players in franchise history chosen to the Pro Bowl.

Along the way, he made a few friends and more than a few enemies. In fact, one newspaper account reports an opposing coach offered $100 to any of his players who knocked Grgich out of a game.

"Shucks, let 'em try," Grgich responded in the 1949 article. "The harder they try, the more tense they become, the more mistakes they make, and the more chance our line has to capitalize on those mistakes."

Grgich is remembered for his ability to light a fire under his teammates with an impassioned locker-room ritual. Before just about every game at Kezar, Grgich would use his forearm to knock a wooden door off its hinges. Then the team would charge through the door onto the field.

"Visco was a wild man," Hall of Fame fullback Joe Perry said. "I had a lot of fun with Visco."

After his career ended, the 49ers still needed his services. Some years later, his former teammate, Albert, was the head coach and had trouble motivating his team. He asked Grgich to pay a visit to the locker room before a game. Grgich, reprising a common scene of the past, knocked the door off its hinges. The 49ers went on to win the game.

"But that was the last time I did it," Grgich said. "My forearm was sore for a month."

Grgich's playing career came to an end after knee surgery at the age of 29. In the second game of the 1952 season, the 49ers were playing the Dallas Texans when Grgich found himself at the wrong place at the wrong time.

Niners defender Al Carapella, Grgich's roommate, grabbed Texans running back Buddy Young, who then swung Carapella around "like a pendulum," Grgich later recalled. "I didn't get out of the way. I had a 250-pound sledge hammer come down on my knee. There was nothing left."

Grgich became a car salesman, but when former coach Buck Shaw found out, he demanded that Grgich get back into the game. So in 1958, Grgich became a football coach while teaching at Oakdale High School.

Grgich continued to be a regular at 49ers games for most of the next four decades. In fact, he was able to experience the euphoria of the organization's first Super Bowl title in January 1982, with a huge assist from his students.

"Being the ultimate 49ers fan and being a teacher and coach at Oakdale, it didn't look like he'd be able to go to the Super Bowl," said Mike Grgich, his son. "But some of the kids found out and they started a collection. They basically paid for his trip to Detroit to watch the Super Bowl."

Grgich has encountered many hardships in the years that followed. But, as Mike says, "He's doing quite well for being 80 years old and 300 pounds."

Grgich suffered a stroke in 1988. Although it did not affect him too much physically, it limited his speech. "He knew what he wanted to say, but it would come out of his mouth in a different way."

In June 2001, his wife of more than 50 years died after a six-month battle with cancer. Grgich met the former Sue Johnston when he was living in San Francisco. She was a talented country singer who was known as "Sioux City Sue."

"After she died, he moved to assisted living," Mike said. "She had hospice and they spent more time with him than her. He was a trooper."

JOHN WOUDENBERG

John Woudenberg was a sophomore in a Denver high school when he saw his first football game. The following spring, he went out for the team.

"Before I even put on a jock, the coach got us all in a room and talked to us for an hour," Woudenberg said. "The only thing I remember from that one hour is when he told us, 'If you hit them harder than they hit you, you won't get hurt.'"

That philosophy, instilled in Woudenberg early, carried him through his football career.

When the Super Bowl was played in Tempe, Arizona, in January 1996, Woudenberg attended a function with many former players. In a group about 30 feet away was former Cleveland Browns fullback Marion Motley, a Hall of Famer.

"Woudenberg," Motley called out, "you hit me as hard as I've ever been hit. When I look at you, it still hurts."

Woudenberg smiled. It was a great way to be remembered from a career that saw him play three seasons with the Pittsburgh Steelers, three years with St. Mary's Pre-Flight during World War II, and the first four seasons of the fledgling 49ers.

"I played offense, defense and special teams," Woudenberg said. "I was probably the only 49er to play 60 minutes, gun to gun."

Woudenberg signed with the 49ers after playing at St. Mary's Pre-Flight, where he was an athletic officer in the Navy. He was named to the All-America Football Conference first team in both 1947 and 1948.

"If it weren't for the Cleveland Browns, we would've been the best thing since sliced bread," said Woudenberg, who lives in Scottsdale, Arizona.

"Paul Brown had a scout on us every game. They had [Dante] Lavelli and [Mac] Speedie, two six-foot-five ends, and we'd have [John] Strzykalski, a 5-10 back, and so they'd just have Otto Graham thread the needle. We'd have to send linebackers out to cover those ends, and then they'd run big Marion Motley up the middle."

In four seasons as AAFC rivals, the 49ers defeated the Browns just twice in nine meetings. In the league title game in 1949, the Browns won the championship with a 21-7 victory over the 49ers at Kezar Stadium.

Woudenberg's biggest contribution to the future of the 49ers came when he told team owner Tony Morabito about this fullback he had been observing while assisting with the Alameda Naval Air Station team. His name was Joe Perry.

JOHN WOUDENBERG

Offensive tackle, defensive line · Denver · Ht. 6-3; Wt. 227
Born: May 25, 1918 · 49ers career: 1946-1949

Career highlights: Broke into NFL in 1940 with Pittsburgh
Steelers, playing three seasons · Played on first 49ers team in
1946 · Second-team All-AAFC in 1947 · First-team All-AAFC
in 1948 · Honorable-mention All-AAFC in 1949.

Author Dave Newhouse writes in *The Million Dollar Backfield* that when Morabito asked Woudenberg about Perry, Woudenberg answered, "Just give him the ball and point him in the right direction."

Obviously, Perry has fond memories of Woudenberg.

"John was a hell of a person and a hell of a player," Perry said.

Woudenberg said he could have continued to play for the 49ers, but after the 1949 season he determined he could provide better for his family if he were in a different line of work. When he broke into professional football with the Steelers in 1940, all linemen made $125 a game. At the time he got out of football, Woudenberg was one of pro football's highest-paid tackles at $9,000 a season.

But he knew he could make a lot more money selling cars, and that is what he did. He moved to Los Angeles, where he became a manager of a dealership. After a few years, he said he was ready to become his own boss, so he bought a Pontiac dealership in Mesa, Arizona.

The dealership was selling five cars a month, but after affordable and effective air conditioning had been developed, Arizona became more than just a seasonable place for people to live. Within three years, his dealership was selling 35 cars a month.

After 10 years, Woudenberg sold the dealership and bought a business that rented barricades, detour signs and blinker lights to road contractors. He sold the business to his oldest son, Dana, in 1980, and he in turn sold it in 1998.

In the 36 years the business was in the family, they went from billing contractors $30,000 a year to $30 million, Woudenberg said.

He still works part time and is involved in four charitable organizations. And he figures he's one of the very few residents of Arizona who does not play golf.

"Golf is against my religion," Woudenberg said. "I refuse to do stuff that I'm not good at. It's tough not to play golf in Arizona. There are more golf courses here than most places have filling stations."

Woudenberg and his wife, Myrna, have been married since 1943 after meeting at the University of Denver. He went into the Navy a week later. After a 30-day indoctrination, he was asked where he wanted to be stationed.

He chose St. Mary's, which became a haven for some of the great athletes of the era. Basketball legend Hank Luisetti and baseball's Charlie Gehringer, both Hall of Famers in their sports, were athletic officers, as well as Bruce Smith, an All-America running back from Minnesota.

When the war was over, assistant coach Jim Lawson hooked on with the new professional football team and signed a large number of the St. Mary's team with the 49ers, including Frankie Albert and Len Eshmont.

After his playing career was over, Woudenberg said he put his football memorabilia in the closet, because he did not want his sons, Dana and Kevin, to feel pressure to play the sport. Both eventually earned athletic scholarships.

"I ran the family like a football team," Woudenberg said. "We had the boys do chores, and they each had their responsibilities."

BILL "TIGER" JOHNSON

B ill "Tiger" Johnson never held a full-time job outside of football, though he earned extra income during his playing days with some part-time stints selling beer, cars and real estate.

"But basically, I've never done anything outside of football," he says proudly.

Johnson demonstrated all the appearances of a football lifer early in his career. A center, he joined the 49ers in 1948, playing in the All-America Football Conference his first two seasons before the club made the leap to the National Football League.

Early on, things were rough. Johnson got married as he was launching his professional career, and the accommodations for the newlyweds were less than ideal.

"We lived for a short time at the Embassy Hotel in 'The Tenderloin,'" Johnson said of the particularly sketchy part of San Francisco. "The team put us there."

"Oh, it was really awful," said his wife, Dot. "I was so young, and I was afraid to walk down the street. It's a good thing, because it wasn't too good out there."

Johnson, who was born in Tyler, Texas, went on to become a mainstay with the 49ers for two decades as a player and coach. It was during his early years with the 49ers that he was tagged with the memorable nickname.

He broke his left hand in a 1948 preseason game and missed several games because of the cumbersome cast. He was sitting in a bar with teammates Norm Standlee and Nick Susoeff when Johnson declared, "When I get out of this thing, I'm going to come out like a tiger!"

Standlee and Susoeff made sure the name stuck. Years later when Johnson moved on to the Cincinnati Bengals as a coach, he thought he had heard the last of his nickname. But a couple of San Francisco writers, in town for a Giants-Reds baseball game, stopped by training camp.

"One of them said, 'By golly, there's Tiger,' and it started all over again," Johnson said.

Johnson earned trips to the Pro Bowl after the 1952 and 1953 seasons, while playing 95 games in his nine-year career. Fullback Joe "The Jet" Perry was the beneficiary of many of those holes up the middle that Johnson helped create.

When asked which offensive linemen through the years helped pave the way for his Hall of Fame career, Perry said, "I would have to say all of them, starting with Bill Johnson and Bruno Banducci."

Even then, it was apparent to him and some of his teammates Johnson would some day become a football coach.

BILL "TIGER" JOHNSON
Center · Tyler J.C. · Ht. 6-3; Wt. 228
Born: July 14, 1926 · 49ers career: 1948-1956

Career highlights: Played 95 games in nine seasons with the
49ers · Starter first seven seasons the 49ers played in NFL ·
Pro Bowl starter in 1952 and 1953 · First-team All-NFL in
1954 · Second-team All-NFL in 1952, 1953, 1955.

"I kind of had an understanding that once my time as a player was up, I'd move onto the coaching staff," Johnson said.

The 49ers fired coach "Red" Strader after one season (1955) and hired Frankie Albert as the head coach.

"Frank and I were very close friends, so he hired me as his offensive line coach," Johnson said. "I started coaching but I had to come back as a player [in 1956] because of an injury."

His playing career with the 49ers ran from 1948 to 1956. He coached with the 49ers from 1956 to 1967.

"I had 20 years with the 49ers total before they wised up," Johnson quipped.

Johnson coached under Albert, "Red" Hickey and Jack Christiansen before leaving for the expansion Bengals in 1968 when Dick Nolan took over as head coach of the 49ers.

Paul Brown was putting together his first coaching staff for the AFL team when he tracked down Johnson in his New York City hotel room, where he was staying for a coaches' convention. Johnson had already been informed he would not join Nolan's new staff with the 49ers.

"He called me at 6 a.m. one morning and woke me up," Johnson said. "He offered me the job in Cincinnati and I accepted."

Also on that initial Bengals staff, which included six assistant coaches, was tight ends coach Bill Walsh. Johnson and Walsh served together for eight seasons before Brown decided it was time to step down and declare his hand-picked successor.

On New Year's Day in 1976, Brown announced Johnson as the head coach. Walsh, who thought he was going to get the job, was devastated. He left the staff to become head coach at Stanford.

"When Paul decided to retire and chose me, it was another step," Johnson said. "I never looked at it as exciting or earth-shattering. I knew Bill wanted the job, and I recognized he was a great coach, and I wanted him to stay on the staff. But he left [to go to Stanford], and obviously he made the right decision."

Johnson had a promising first season, leading the Bengals to a 10-4 record in 1976. The club went 8-6 in 1977. When the Bengals lost 28-12 to the 49ers at Candlestick Park in 1978 to fall to 0-5, Johnson resigned. It was one of only two victories the 49ers would earn that season.

The whole episode was a turning point in Walsh's career. He acknowledged in a 1999 article in the *Cincinnati Enquirer* that it proved to his advantage to be passed over for the job at that point in his career.

"Who's to say what happened to Tiger wouldn't have happened to me?" Walsh said. "I don't think I was at the maturity level yet. I can see where Paul was coming from. Bill Johnson had been an established player in the league. He'd been a coach.

"Bill and I worked together closely, and I think Paul felt it would still be the same type of situation. But I wanted to move on."

Johnson said he still considers Walsh a very good friend.

The end of Johnson's head-coaching career did not spell the end of his career. He returned to the Bengals coaching staff in 1985 under Sam Wyche. He spent six seasons on his staff before retiring from coaching in 1990 at the age of 64. He spends time in Cincinnati and Florida, where he plays a lot of golf, he said.

"I don't think any person could have enjoyed anything in life as much as I enjoyed playing professional football," Johnson said. "In that time we weren't getting wealthy, but we were very much like a family. I spent a long time with the 49ers. They're pretty much my ballclub. I still root for them."

Where Have You Gone?

JOE "THE JET" PERRY

O ne year after Jackie Robinson broke baseball's color barrier, in the 49ers' third year of existence, Joe "The Jet" Perry became the 49ers' first black player.

And like Robinson, Perry had to endure the racially motivated taunts, epithets and cheap shots that came with the territory in professional sports.

"That's just the way it was," Perry said. "I never let it get to me. I let everything roll off my back."

All that mattered to Perry was that he had the support of owner Tony Morabito and his teammates. Perry fondly recalls having such roommates as Hardy Brown, Y.A. Tittle, Lowell Wagner, and Verl Lillywhite.

But Morabito was Perry's most trusted friend. Morabito scouted Perry, who played for the Alameda Naval Air Station before agreeing to join the 49ers in the 1948 season.

"We had an alliance like father and son," Perry said of Morabito. "We had a trust in each other. I never even signed a contract with him. It was always a handshake deal. I never knew what I was going to make, but I trusted him to take care of me.

"I can't explain things. When we made eye contact for the first time, I knew this would be a person I would love, respect and trust. We never argued about anything."

When Perry became the first 49ers player to rush for more than 1,000 yards in 1953, Morabito generously awarded his star player an extra $5 for every yard gained. The bonus of $5,090 for 1,018 yards rushing was—and still is—greatly appreciated by Perry.

At times when it might have seemed like the world was against him, Perry knew Morabito would be there for him.

"I was one of the few black players in the league, so I'd get the hell kicked out of me," Perry said. "Wherever you went, it was the same thing. It didn't matter whether it was Los Angeles, San Francisco, or anywhere. You got the N-word and all of that stuff. I'd just say, 'Bring it on.' That's what I got from Tony. He'd tell me, 'Whenever they hit you hard, just hit back harder.'"

Author Dave Newhouse relays an anecdote in his book, *The Million Dollar Backfield*, in which Buffalo Bills owner Jim Breuil chastised Morabito for signing Perry, a fullback, prior to their All-America Football Conference regular-season opener in 1948 at Kezar Stadium.

"It makes it tough on all of us who don't sign a Negro," Breuil told Morabito. "Besides, they're troublemakers. Why did you do it, Tony?"

JOE "THE JET" PERRY

Fullback · Compton J.C. · Ht. 6-0; Wt. 203
Born: January 22, 1927 · 49ers career: 1948-1960, 1963

Career highlights: Inducted into Pro Football Hall of Fame in 1969 · First player in NFL history to gain 1,000 yards two consecutive seasons · Team's all-time leading rusher with 7,344 yards with team-record 50 rushing touchdowns · Led 49ers in rushing seven straight seasons (1949-1955) · NFL Player of the Year in 1954 and 1955 · Len Eshmont Award winner in 1958 · Selected to NFL's All-Decade team for the 1950s · Jersey No. 34 retired in 1971 · Played for Baltimore Colts in 1961, 1962, before returning to end career with 49ers.
Played 176 games in 16-year career.

On Perry's first carry of the game, also his first with the 49ers, he blasted around right end for a 58-yard touchdown run. Morabito turned to Breuil and shot back, "That's why, Jim."

Longtime offensive tackle Bob St. Clair said Perry's skin color was never an issue with his teammates.

"We didn't have those prejudices," St. Clair said. "All the guys from the south that we'd draft, when they got to the team they'd immediately know that none of that was tolerated. We were a team. We didn't care if you were blue, green, or orange."

St. Clair recalls his first road trip with the 49ers in 1953. He sat next to Perry on the flight and asked where they should go that evening in Baltimore. Perry avoided answering, and St. Clair said, "I'll call you later in your room."

When Perry said he was not staying in the team hotel but a private house, St. Clair said, "How do you get that luxury? I have to stay in a hotel."

What St. Clair figured out later was that Perry was not allowed to stay in the team hotel. "That's how naïve I was," St. Clair said.

Morabito did his best to make sure Perry was treated with the respect he deserved. When asked in 2003 about what he remembers most about Kezar Stadium, Perry did not detail any of the good times he had on that field. His most vivid memory was of the tragic events of October 27, 1957.

On that day, Morabito died of a heart attack in the first half of a game against the Chicago Bears. Perry played the second half in tears, and the 49ers forged a come-from-behind victory.

Morabito left such a mark on Perry, that when he entered the Pro Football Hall of Fame in 1969, Josephine Morabito, Tony's widow, was his presenter.

Despite sharing carries with Hall of Famers Hugh McElhenny and John Henry Johnson for much of his time with the 49ers, Perry still managed to put up some unbelievable numbers.

He had 18 career 100-yard rushing games, still a 49ers record. And he averaged 13.4 yards a carry in one game, gaining 174 yards on 13 carries in a 24-21 victory over the Detroit Lions in 1958.

In 1953 and 1954, Perry became the first player in NFL history to record back-to-back 1,000-yard seasons. He was the league's all-time leading rusher before Jim Brown surged past him.

Perry gained 2,379 yards in two seasons in the AAFC, which the 49ers do not count as part of his career rushing total. Even without those yards, Perry is still the team's all-time leading rusher with 7,344 yards. No one in 49ers history has surpassed "The Jet."

Frankie Albert gave Perry his nickname. Albert coined the moniker out of frustration while trying to hand off to Perry during a practice his rookie season.

"It was the first year that the jet airplane came out," Perry recalls. "We were taking handoffs. We were running our 30 and 31 F Trap, which is the fullback up the middle. Frankie was under center, and he would turn to hand me the ball, and I'd be past him. He'd say, 'Damn, you're cheating.' And I told him, 'No, I'm not.'

"I told him, 'Frankie, you got to get quicker.' And he said, 'Perry is like a jet.'"

The only thing that could ground Perry was a dearth of carries. In 1958, he averaged 6.1 yards a carry but rushed for 758 yards because his number was called on just 125 of the team's 359 rushing attempts that season.

The next year, Howard "Red" Hickey replaced Perry's old friend, Albert, as head coach of the 49ers. Perry said his experience playing for Hickey was forgettable. In 1961, he was sent to the Baltimore Colts, where he spent the next two seasons.

Perry returned to San Francisco in 1963 to finish his career with the 49ers, at the request of Tony's brother, Vic Morabito.

He worked for the 49ers as a special-teams coach in 1968, then was re-assigned as a scout. He stayed with the 49ers until 1974, but now says he wants nothing to do with his former team.

Perry now lives in Chandler, Arizona, with Donna, his wife of more than 20 years. He plays golf and just recently began bowling again after a 10-year hiatus. Perry used to own a bowling supplies store in San Francisco.

"My wife says, 'You get so mad,'" said Perry, who averages in the 180s. "That's just the competitiveness in me. I compete at everything I do, whether it's ping-pong, tiddlywinks or bowling."

PAUL
SALATA

There's nothing irrelevant about Paul Salata, who played end for the 49ers during the transition from the All-America Football Conference to the National Football League.

Although he played just one and a half seasons with the 49ers, he holds a special place in team lore. He scored the 49ers' final touchdown in the AAFC and the first touchdown when the organization joined the NFL.

Salata also played three seasons in the Canadian Football League, but his most lasting contribution to the professional game is apparent every year during the NFL Draft. Salata takes the stage in an annual tradition to announce the final pick in the draft—a distinction he coined, "Mr. Irrelevant."

"I spent a lot of time in a supporting role while playing football," Salata said. "Sometimes I was the runner-up, and sometimes I was the starter and had a guy behind me. But I've always liked the team concept of football. Everybody is equal, in my mind. Everybody on the team is essential."

Approximately 50 years ago, Salata recalls some people in the Newport Beach area of Southern California would pick an individual out of a phone book and name a day after that person. One year, someone from St. Louis was chosen and flown out to California in a random act of kindness.

That memory stuck with Salata, who decided to apply the same sentiment toward the draft. After all, the No. 1 pick in the draft received all the attention and adoration. But what about the player chosen with the final pick? What ever happened to him?

Salata spoke with the late Pete Rozelle, NFL commissioner, about his idea to bestow all kinds of attention and gifts onto the last pick in the draft. The commissioner thought it was a good idea.

In 1976, 487 players were selected in the 17-round draft. Kelvin Kirk, a receiver from Dayton, was the first Mr. Irrelevant when he became property of the Pittsburgh Steelers. Salata wanted to bring Kirk to Newport Beach for a week of fun.

"He had some concerns because he had never heard of it," Salata said, "so I called Mr. [Art] Rooney, and I had old man Rooney call the kid and say, 'If Salata says it's good, it's good.'"

The very first year did not go as planned. Kirk missed his flight, so that left Salata scrambling to find someone to sit on a float to represent him for the parade in his honor.

"We needed some guy who looked like a football player," Salata said. "We didn't have many African-Americans in our town, but there was one guy who worked at the supermarket. We put him in the parade."

PAUL SALATA
End · Southern California · Ht. 6-2; Wt. 191
Born: October 17, 1926 · 49ers career: 1949-50

Career highlights: Scored 49ers' final touchdown in All-America
Football Conference, as well as first TD in NFL · Played 22
games in two-year NFL career, including seven with Baltimore
Colts in 1950 after midseason trade.

"We even put the fake guy up on the podium, and he was answering all the questions at the press conference. In the middle of that, here came the real football player, so we made the switch and just went on as if nothing ever happened."

Through the years, Salata and his team of helpers, led by daughter Melanie, have gotten things to run a lot smoother. His entire family has been involved, including his wife of 52 years, Beverly, who passed away more than two years ago.

Usually, the last week of June is reserved for "Irrelevant Week." The honoree comes to Newport Beach on a Sunday night, and the arrival party happens on Monday. Typically, a thousand people attend the party, and the Newport Beach Chamber of Commerce is involved.

The last pick in the draft is showered with gifts, including jerseys from each of the 32 teams in the league and a Rolex watch. He is also awarded the anti-Heisman Trophy, called—you guessed it—the Lowsman Trophy. Instead of the figure on the trophy striking the Heisman pose, the Lowsman figure is fumbling the football.

The next day is the parade at Disneyland, where "Mr. Irrelevant" is the grand marshal. To round out the week, there is usually a banquet, a yachting regatta, and a pub crawl. On Saturday, the football hopeful is delivered to the NFL rookie symposium, which takes place in the San Diego area.

Irrelevant Week was scheduled for its 30th anniversary in June. Perhaps the most memorable occurred in 1996 when the 49ers selected linebacker Sam Manuel of New Mexico State with the final pick, just a few spots after taking his twin brother, tight end Sean Manuel. The Manuels both took part in the festivities, which included their arrival at the kickoff party on a tandem bike.

Salata recalls what it is like to be fawned over. When he arrived in San Francisco after a standout career at Southern California, he routinely received free meals at some of the fine restaurants in North Beach, because they thought he was Italian.

But one day, a San Francisco newspaper blew his cover. A story about Salata ran with the headline "Serbian Prince Starts for 49ers" and those privileges came to an abrupt end.

"When they found out I was Yugoslavian, they cut off my free dinners," he said.

Salata remembers the 1949 AAFC championship game against the powerful Cleveland Browns, a team the 49ers upset 56-28 in the regular season. Because the league was struggling, it did not appear as if the players would be paid for the title game.

"There were no provisions to pay us, so we went on strike for 24 hours," Salata said. "[John] Woudenberg and those guys said, 'We're not going to play for nothing.' We went on with it anyhow."

The 49ers lost 21-7, with Salata scoring the team's only touchdown on a 23-yard pass from Frankie Albert with :14 remaining. The loser's share was a paltry $142 apiece. "Even by those standards, it was pretty skinny," he said.

Albert and Salata also hooked up for the 49ers' first touchdown in the NFL, a 17-yard scoring play in the second quarter of a 21-17 loss to the New York Yankees.

After his career was completed, Salata worked primarily in the rock and gravel business. He still maintains a real estate office but cut back from working full time in 1985.

CLAY MATTHEWS

The genes he passed down to his famous sons suggest Clay Matthews could have played at least another decade in professional football.

But the Georgia Tech graduate had gone through enough as the team captain of the 49ers in 1955 that he was ready to retire after being sent in a trade to the Philadelphia Eagles. So after playing just four seasons in the NFL, the South Carolina native put his degree to work as an industrial engineer.

Things turned out pretty well for Matthews, who became an ultra-successful businessman.

Matthews left the long football careers to his sons, Clay Jr. and Bruce.

Each played a remarkable 19 seasons in the NFL. Clay, a linebacker, went to four Pro Bowls during his career with the Cleveland Browns and Atlanta Falcons. Bruce, a versatile offensive lineman, was selected to the Pro Bowl 14 times while playing his entire career with the Houston Oilers/Tennessee Titans organization. He is considered a certain Hall of Famer.

There is no telling how their father's career would have turned out if he had remained in the NFL, though he's certain he would not have lasted 19 seasons.

"My sons were different than me. They didn't hang out in bars and chase women," Matthews said, punctuating his remarks with an infectious laugh. "They're both good Christian guys. They behave themselves. They don't drink. They go to church."

The elder Matthews was held in high regard by his teammates. He was a born leader whom his peers selected to act as the buffer between the players and team management.

The 49ers were going through all kinds of internal strife during Matthews's days as a captain. Lawrence "Buck" Shaw, the only head coach since the franchise was formed in 1946 was let go after the 49ers finished with a 7-4-1 record in 1954.

In came taskmaster Norman "Red" Strader, and chaos ensued. Despite a roster loaded with talent, the 49ers sunk to a disappointing 4-8 record in 1955. Strader was fired after the season, replaced by Frankie Albert.

"We had all kinds of team problems," Matthews said. "Red Strader was the coach, and I was the captain of the team, through no choice of my own. All the gripes and things that happened, I had to present to management. All of a sudden at the end of the year, we had a losing season. Red Strader was gone, and Clay Matthews, the troublemaker, was still the captain of the team."

**Career highlights: Began career with 49ers as right tackle ·
Switched to defensive end in 1953 · Team captain ·
Played 45 games in four-year career.**

Perhaps as a portend, Matthews's picture does not appear on the 49ers' 1955 team photo.

"They traded me to Philadelphia, and I didn't want to start all over," Matthews said. "I just retired. I was making $7,000 a year, and I had two kids. I eventually had seven, so I guess it was a good thing I got out."

Matthews started at General Telephone and rose through the ranks to become the manager of industrial engineering. He also worked for ITT in Raleigh, North Carolina, and later owned a business that made citizen-band radios.

Hamilton Beach later hired him, and one of his first moves was to close down a plant in Racine, Wisconsin, and moved it into two plants in North Carolina.

"I came to be known affectionately by the name I carried for the rest of my career," he said, "that 'Son of a Bitch from South Carolina.' "

He became president of several large companies through the rest of his career, which ended with his retirement in 1993.

"I worked in Chicago; Northern California; Southern California; three different places in Canada; London; Racine; Jackson, Michigan; Amarillo, Texas, and Raleigh, North Carolina," Matthews said. "I bought and sold 28 homes."

Clay Matthews was quite a businessman, but his attempt at becoming an agent for one of his sons wasn't quite as successful. In 1983, Bruce was the Oilers' No. 1 draft pick out of Southern California.

"I said, 'Bruce, do you have an agent?' He said no," Matthews said. "I said, 'Would you like for me to be your agent?' He said, 'Well, you've done a pretty good job in the business world, how much money did you make in football?'

"I told him I made $42,000. He said, 'Forty-two thousand a year in the 1950s was a lot of money.' I said, 'Bruce, that was $42,000 for six years.'

"Bruce said, 'I think I'm going to get another agent.'"

While all his children gave him a multitude of special times, he looks back fondly on the experience of raising mentally handicapped twins Brad and Raymond. Brad died in 2003 after being hit by a truck in Arcadia, California.

"My son Bruce and his wife, Carrie, just had his seventh child, and she has Down Syndrome," Matthews said. "He came to me and said, 'What am I going to do?' I said, 'What do you mean? What did I do when God gave me two handicapped children?' He said, 'You raised them.' So I said, 'What's the big deal? You should know exactly how to do it.'"

Matthews said the experience of having two children with special needs supplied him and his family with constant lessons in life.

"Bruce and Clay never let them quit at anything they did," Matthews said. "They were both state champions in swimming for the Special Olympics."

Clay Matthews lives in Charleston, South Carolina, with Carolyn, his wife of more than 20 years. His first wife, Daisy, with whom he was married 32 years, passed away in 1984 from cancer.

In 2003, he underwent prostrate surgery and endured 37 radiation treatments. He had two feet of his colon removed and underwent triple-bypass heart surgery.

"Now, I'm fine," he said. "I've been blessed."

BILLY
WILSON

Even during the days of "The Million Dollar Backfield," the 49ers had plenty of options through the air.

The organization's first receiver to make a league-wide impact was Billy Wilson, who established himself as one of the best pass-catchers of the decade. For most of the 1950s, Wilson was on equal footing with such Hall of Fame receivers as Raymond Berry, Tom Fears, and Elroy "Crazylegs" Hirsch.

Certainly, a convincing argument can be made that Wilson belongs in the Pro Football Hall of Fame.

To wit, Philadelphia Eagles receiver Pete Pihos caught 373 passes for 5,619 yards during his nine-year career that spanned 1947 to '55. He led the league in receiving three times.

Wilson also led the league in receiving three times during his 10-year career from 1951 to 1960. He caught 407 passes for 5,902 yards and 49 touchdowns. Pihos was elected into the Hall of Fame in 1970. Wilson is still waiting.

Niners Hall of Fame coach Bill Walsh has taken up the cause of trying to get Wilson inducted into the Canton, Ohio, shrine.

"He was the best receiver in the league and led the league in receiving," Walsh said. "He was MVP of the Pro Bowl, when that game meant something. He was one of the most admired players and respected players in football."

Walsh has campaigned for Wilson to be inducted into the Hall of Fame, but so far the 39-member board of selectors has not budged. "I've done everything I can do," Walsh said.

He added, "I've thought that Billy should have been enshrined years ago. He deserves it as much as a lot of people who have gotten into the Hall of Fame, myself included."

When Wilson retired after the 1960 season, only Green Bay's Don Hutson had caught more passes than he did in league history. And remember, the 49ers were primarily a running team for most of the 1950s behind Joe Perry, Hugh McElhenny, and John Henry Johnson.

In fact, the 49ers had six players from the 1950s who would ultimately be inducted into the Hall of Fame. In addition to Perry, McElhenny and Johnson, the 49ers also boasted quarterback Y.A. Tittle and linemen Leo Nomellini and Bob St. Clair.

But Wilson is the only 49ers player during that time to earn six consecutive trips to the Pro Bowl. He was selected to the game every season from 1954 to 1959. On January

BILLY WILSON
END   SAN FRANCISCO 49'ERS

BILLY WILSON
End · San Jose State · Ht. 6-3; Wt. 191
Born: February 3, 1927 · 49ers career: 1951-1960

Career highlights: Selected in 22nd round of 1950 draft ·
Named to Pro Bowl six consecutive seasons (1954-1959) · Led
league in touchdown catches (10) in 1953 · Led league in
receptions in 1954, 1956 and 1957 · Finished career with 407
catches for 5,902 yards and 49 touchdowns ·
MVP of the Pro Bowl in 1955.

16, 1955, he was named the Player of the Game, as the West chalked up a 26-19 victory over the East at the Los Angeles Memorial Coliseum.

Known for his consistency, Wilson's biggest statistical day came in a 34-23 loss to the Chicago Bears in 1955 when he caught eight passes for 192 yards. Two years later he played an important role in perhaps the most emotional regular-season game in franchise history. On the day popular owner Tony Morabito collapsed and died of a heart attack in 1957, the inspired 49ers rallied from a 10-point deficit to pull out a 21-17 victory over the Bears on Wilson's fourth-quarter scoring catch from Tittle.

Even with the rules changes making it easier for teams to pass the football, Wilson's statistics are still among the best in 49ers history. He ranks sixth all-time in receptions, fifth in receiving yards and fourth in touchdowns, behind only Jerry Rice, Terrell Owens and Gene Washington.

After his career concluded, Wilson remained a 49ers employee for 30 years in coaching, scouting, and public relations. He coached receivers in 1961 and 1962, came back to coach from 1964 to 1967, and again in 1980.

There were long odds against Wilson sticking around for very long when he arrived on the scene in 1950. Wilson, who played his college ball at San Jose State, was chosen in the 22nd round of the draft. Moreover, the 49ers had already selected six players at his position prior to making the selection.

Wilson remained active during his retirement, but he received a jolt in 2004 when he was diagnosed with colon cancer.

"I had two major surgeries and a couple other procedures," said Wilson, who joined many of his former teammates for the 49ers' alumni weekend gathering in October 2004. "I lost a lot of weight, but I'm fine now."

Wilson, who played at six-foot-three, 190 pounds, said he lost 14 pounds during his battle with cancer. "Fourteen pounds is a lot for me," he said. "I looked like [a survivor of] the Bataan Death March."

Wilson lives in San Diego for about six months out of the year. He had expected to live there to be near his two daughters and his six grandchildren. But in the mid-1990s, he took a vacation in the Feather River Canyon and found a new part-time home.

"We went up there a couple summers and really liked it," he said. "I have a home on the golf course at White Hawk Ranch in a little town called Clio, and we kept the house we bought in San Diego. It works great. I can go back and forth."

Where Have You Gone?

Y.A.
TITTLE

Y.A. Tittle spent 17 seasons in the NFL, putting together a Hall of Fame career that included two MVP seasons. However, he began laying the groundwork for his life outside of football in his first few seasons with the 49ers.

In 1955, Tittle entered the insurance business as a way to supplement his paltry football salary. "Oh, yeah, we all had to get another job in those years," Tittle said. "They paid us with blue-chip stamps, so it was tough to live on our football salary. We all had other jobs."

More than a half-century later, Tittle is still involved in the insurance business. Y.A. Tittle and Associates has five offices in Northern California: Mountain View, Half Moon Bay, San Jose, Modesto and Grass Valley.

Of course, Tittle was the quarterback during a time when the 49ers boasted a backfield of four future Hall of Famers, including Joe Perry, Hugh McElhenny, and John Henry Johnson. In Dave Newhouse's fine book, *The Million Dollar Backfield*, he writes, "Tittle is the only member of the Million Dollar Backfield to become a multimillionaire, profiting from an insurance business he prospered from after football."

When asked how active he remains in the business, Tittle replies, "I go up there and second-guess them and then go home around lunch time."

For many years the only thing second-guessed was the trade that sent Tittle from the 49ers to the New York Giants. After eight consecutive seasons as the 49ers' leading passer, the team traded him in 1961 to the Giants for journeyman guard/linebacker Lou Cordileone.

Cordileone spent only one season with the 49ers while Tittle was putting the finishing touches on his Hall of Fame career. He was named NFL Most Valuable Player in 1961 and 1963. And in 1962 he threw 33 touchdown passes and a career-high 3,224 yards.

Tittle maintained his permanent residence in the Bay Area, as his wife, Minnette, would visit New York and bring the kids for about a month every season. The Tittles were married in December 1948.

He is the only player in professional football history drafted in the first round three times. The Cleveland Browns selected him in the first round of the All-America Football Conference draft in 1948. That same year, the Detroit Lions of the NFL chose him with the sixth overall selection.

Tittle signed with the Browns but never played for them, with future Hall of Famer Otto Graham already flourishing in Cleveland. The AAFC commissioner awarded Tittle

Y.A. TITTLE
Quarterback · Louisiana State · Ht. 6-0; Wt. 182
Born: October 24, 1926 · 49ers career: 1951-1960

Career highlights: Inducted into Pro Football Hall of Fame in
1971 · Drafted in the first round three times, including by
49ers in 1951 · Pro Bowl in 1953, 1954 and 1957 while with
49ers · Winner of the first Len Eshmont Award in 1957 ·
Traded to N.Y. Giants in 1961 · Won NFL MVP Award in
1961 and 1963 · Played 201 games in 17 seasons ·
Began career with Baltimore Colts in 1948.

to the Baltimore Colts in an effort to balance the league. After the original Colts folded after a onc-ycar run in the NFL, Tittle was again eligible for the draft in 1951.

That is when the 49ers selected him and kept him for 10 up-and-down seasons.

The 49ers never gave Tittle much reason to feel secure during his time with them. In 1954 they selected quarterback Bernie Faloney of Maryland with the No. 10 overall pick; in 1956 they took quarterback Earl Morrall of Michigan State with the second overall pick; and in 1957 they chose John Brodie of Stanford with the second pick in the first round.

The 49ers selected almost entirely offensive players in the early rounds of their drafts through the 1950s, generally at positions where they already had established players.

Tittle helped put the 49ers on the national sporting map. In 1954, the first year of *Sports Illustrated*, Tittle became the organization's first representative to grace a cover.

Initially Tittle shared time with Frankie Albert, whose career was winding down. From 1953 to 1955, he was the starting quarterback but Morrall took some of his snaps in 1956.

Brodie attempted just 21 passes as a rookie in 1957, as Tittle put together an outstanding season and was named UPI's NFL Player of the Year. Tittle and Brodie split time from 1958 to 1960, opening the door for the 49ers to trade Tittle to the Giants.

After years of putting up with the fickle fans at Kezar Stadium, Tittle went to New York at the age of 35 and showed he still had a lot left.

Tittle's greatest year in the pros came in 1963, leading the league with 221 completions in 367 attempts for 3,145 yards. His 36 touchdown passes still stand as the Giants' single-season record. Tittle played in six Pro Bowls, including three during his time with the 49ers.

He has also been an immense success outside of football, though he still admits to missing the thrill of strapping on the pads every Sunday.

"I miss football, obviously," Tittle said. "I think everybody does who played it as long as I did. I started the insurance business while I was still playing, so that helps. I'd go right from the end of the season into something else, so I was able to learn another line of work."

Born in October 1926, Tittle was christened with the unique name Yelberton Abraham Tittle Jr.

"I've been called Y.A. ever since I can remember," Tittle said in Newhouse's book, "except when I got married. The preacher got confused and said, 'Do you, Wayne, take this woman?"

Tittle was called a lot of other names, too, with nicknames of "Ya-Ya" and "The Bald Eagle."

Explains former 49ers offensive tackle Len Rohde: "The interesting thing is that Y.A. never changed. He looked like he was 50 even when he was 25."

HUGH "THE KING" McELHENNY

In the case of Hugh McElhenny, the stat sheet *always* lied.

He finished his 13-year NFL career rushing for 5,281 yards and catching passes for another 3,247. But his 8,528 total yards from scrimmage is a bit misleading, because his zig-zag running style—think of an exaggerated Barry Sanders—certainly meant he covered a lot more ground than that with the football in his hands.

"They used to say, 'McElhenny will run 50 yards to get 10,'" he said.

His remarkable open-field running style enabled him to average 4.9 yards a carry through his nine seasons with the 49ers.

McElhenny was a big play waiting to happen. He owns three of the four longest runs from scrimmage in 49ers' history with touchdown sprints of 89 and 82 yards against the Dallas Texans in 1952 and an 86-yarder at Green Bay in 1956. Only Garrison Hearst's 96-yard touchdown romp in overtime against the New York Jets in the 1998 season opener ranks ahead of McElhenny's longest runs in team history.

Moreover, his 94-yard punt return against Chicago in 1952 stood as the team's standard for 36 years until John Taylor returned a punt 95 yards for a touchdown against Washington in 1988.

After that game, a nickname was born. Quarterback Frankie Albert entered the locker room with the game ball and announced McElhenny was the "king of the halfbacks."

McElhenny was considered akin to royalty at the University of Washington before joining the 49ers in 1952 as a first-round draft pick. But he certainly was not afforded any special treatment when he met 49ers executive Vic Morabito to talk about his first contract.

Niners quarterback Frankie Albert had become a mentor to McElhenny, and he advised him to ask the team for nothing less than $30,000 for his rookie contract. Morabito met McElhenny for lunch at the Sheraton on Wilshire Boulevard in Los Angeles.

"I didn't know Vic, but he seemed to be the guy responsible for signing me—I wish it would've been Tony [Morabito] because he was the real neat owner of that group," McElhenny said. "Anyway, we were chatting it up and he asked, 'What would it take to sign you?'"

When McElhenny said $30,000, an exorbitant figure for those days, Vic Morabito said he couldn't pay that big of a sum.

HUGH "THE KING" McELHENNY
Halfback · Washington · Ht. 6-1; Wt. 197
Born: December 31, 1928 · 49ers career: 1952-1960

Career highlights: Inducted into Pro Football Hall of Fame in 1970 · Selected in first round of 1952 draft · First-team All-NFL in 1952, 1953 · Second-team All-NFL in 1954, 1956, 1957 · Selected on the NFL's All-Decade team for the 1950s · Also played for Minnesota Vikings (1961 and 1962), New York Giants (1963) and Detroit Lions (1964) · Jersey No. 39 retired 1971 · Played 143 games in 13-year pro career.

"He excused himself to go to the john," McElhenny said, "and he never came back. I got stuck for the lunch tab, and I ended up signing for $7,000."

McElhenny proved to be worth every penny. In 1952, the 49ers were up for sale, but with the help of one of the game's most exciting players, they were eventually taken off the market. He was named *Sport Magazine's* NFL Player of the Year, All-Pro, and NFL Rookie of the Year.

McElhenny probably could have set all kinds of rushing records if he were on another team. He led the team in carries just twice during his nine seasons with the club, because he shared the backfield with the likes of Joe Perry, John Henry Johnson and, later, J.D. Smith.

After clashing with head coach Howard "Red" Hickey in 1960, McElhenny was looking to leave the 49ers. He was eventually sent to the Minnesota Vikings, averaging 4.8 yards a carry in 1961. He finished his career with the New York Giants and Detroit Lions. He entered the Pro Football Hall of Fame in 1970.

McElhenny played for three teams after the 49ers, and that diluted his ties to his first team. Moreover, he said many of the 49ers old-timers felt neglected during Eddie DeBartolo's ownership era, as the bad feelings still existed from the Joe Thomas era as general manager.

McElhenny, whose jersey No. 39 the 49ers retired in 1971, feels more of a link to football in Seattle, where he lived until moving to Henderson, Nevada, in 1997. McElhenny takes a large measure of pride in helping create enthusiasm for bringing an NFL franchise to Seattle in 1976.

Had things worked out differently three decades ago, the 49ers might be in the NFC West with the Seattle Kings instead of the Seahawks.

The first proposed ownership group that tried to win an NFL expansion club for Seattle worked under the name of royalty, which was appropriate considering the central figure was none other than Hugh "The King" McElhenny.

"He will tell you 'Kings' came from King County and the Kingdome," said Seahawks vice president/administration Gary Wright, one of three people who have been with the organization since its inception.

"But I really believe it was because of his nickname. Hugh McElhenny was huge in Seattle. His celebrity up here was big."

It all started when Minnesota businessman Wayne Field tried to put together a group to win an expansion club for the Emerald City. McElhenny had never heard of Field before receiving a phone call from him one day.

If anybody in Seattle could create a buzz about football, it was McElhenny. And if anybody in Seattle knew about the NFL, it was McElhenny.

In the mid-1960s, McElhenny worked for an advertising agency in San Francisco that had a contract to represent NFL Properties. His job was to travel the country, calling on corporations to use football as a means to sell their products and services.

"The reason Wayne Field chose me was because of my background of playing the game of football, working with the advertising agency, and my popularity of being an All-American at the University of Washington," McElhenny said.

"I also had an indication the NFL was going to expand; they were going to be forced to expand. [NFL Commissioner] Pete Rozelle wanted to go from 26 to 28 teams, and Seattle was the 14th largest market."

McElhenny used his influence and popularity to bring two NFL exhibition games to Husky Stadium, one of them involving Joe Namath's New York Jets against Terry Bradshaw's Pittsburgh Steelers in 1972.

"We turned in our financial program to the league, and they never said anything," McElhenny said. "All of a sudden, in 1974, the Nordstrom group put in a bid that was real strong, and their financial program was accepted over ours. They deserved it.

"We could've put the money together, partly because we were going to make season-ticket holders 49 percent part of the ownership."

McElhenny said his group would have hired Johnny Thompson as its general manager. Thompson had formerly worked in the athletic department at Washington and held several NFL jobs, including with the league office in New York.

Instead, the Nordstrom group hired Thompson, and McElhenny called New York to set up a meeting with Thompson to see if he could join the newly formed organization.

"He said he'd be out [to Seattle] in a couple weeks," McElhenny said. "I never heard from him again."

McElhenny, one of the members of the 49ers' famed "Million Dollar Backfield," would be a multimillionaire today if his group had won the bid. The Nordstroms paid $16 million for the Seahawks. In 1988, the department store family sold to Bay Area developer Ken Behring for $99 million. The Seahawks are currently valued at $712 million, according to *Forbes* magazine.

Professional football is undergoing a rebirth in Seattle, with a new stadium and an improved team. McElhenny, meanwhile, is largely a forgotten man despite laying most of the groundwork more than 30 years ago.

"I don't think anybody in Seattle or the original owners gave me or Wayne Field the credit we deserved," he said. "We kept it in front of the NFL for three years. We kept telling them, 'This was a place to come when you expand.' We take credit for that."

McElhenny ended up working for Pepsi-Cola in Seattle until his retirement in 1995. That year, he nearly lost his life to a nerve disorder called Guillain-Barre Syndrome, which afflicts one in 100,000 people. He was temporarily paralyzed from the neck down and his weight dropped from 210 to 145.

"It took me a year to get rid of my walker," he said. Although he has made nearly a full recovery, McElhenny is only frustrated these days because he can't break 90 on the golf course.

BOB
St. CLAIR

Nobody played more football games at Kezar Stadium than Bob St. Clair.
The San Francisco native attended Polytechnic High School, which has since closed. The school played its games across the street at Kezar. He also played college ball at the University of San Francisco, which was a powerhouse before disbanding the program. Again, his home field was Kezar.

Then when he was certain he would be playing in the NFL for the Los Angeles Rams, the 49ers swooped in and selected St. Clair in the third round of the 1953 draft.

St. Clair played 189 games at Kezar Stadium in 19 high school, college and professional seasons. In 2001, the field—still being used for high school games—was fittingly dedicated in his honor.

It has been an amazing ride for St. Clair, who retired in 1964 after tearing both Achilles' tendons in three years. Twenty-six years after his career came to an end, St. Clair received the ultimate validation for any football player.

St. Clair was inducted into the Pro Football Hall of Fame, joining four offensive teammates from that era: running backs Joe Perry, Hugh McElhenny and John Henry Johnson, and quarterback Y.A. Tittle.

"The thing to realize is that the 49ers have three running backs and a quarterback from those teams already in the hall," receiver Billy Wilson told the *San Francisco Chronicle* in 1990. "Someone had to be doing the blocking."

More than a decade later, St. Clair received another stream of honors. In 2001, the City of San Francisco and the Recreation and Parks Department named the Kezar turf "Bob St. Clair Field." Later that year the 49ers retired St. Clair's No. 79, though six players had worn it since he retired.

"I've had so many highlights, so how do you say which one is best?" St. Clair said. "I went into the Hall of Fame; I had my jersey retired by my hometown team; they named the field at Kezar after me. And I'm still alive to enjoy it."

St. Clair still cuts an imposing figure more than four decades after his retirement. He was a behemoth in his day, standing six foot nine and weighing 265 pounds. And his idiosyncratic personality was just as large.

Upon joining the 49ers in 1953, the club's veterans nicknamed him "Geek," because of his affinity for raw meat. In the old days of the carnival sideshow, a person who bit the heads off live chickens was called a geek.

BOB St. CLAIR

Offensive tackle · San Francisco/Tulsa · Ht. 6-9; Wt. 265
Born: February 18, 1931 · 49ers career: 1953-1963

Career highlights: Inducted into Pro Football Hall of Fame in 1990 · Selected in third round of 1953 draft · Pro Bowl in 1956, 1958, 1959, 1960 and 1961 · First-team All-NFL in 1955, 1956 and 1960 · Blocked 10 field goals and extra points in 1956 · Len Eshmont Award winner in 1963 · Selected on the NFL's All-Decade team for the 1950s · Jersey No. 79 retired in 2001 · Played 119 games in 11-year career.

When he was a child, St. Clair's grandmother fed him raw meat. St. Clair ate everything raw—and he's been denied service at more than one restaurant through the years because of his unusual preference.

Only once, he says, did his stomach revolt. In the early 1960s he ate some bad raw chicken livers and threw up. "Naturally, I haven't eaten chicken livers since," he said.

St. Clair enjoys every kind of meat raw. He has been places where it was appropriate for him to eat steak that has been cooked, but he just can't force himself to go all the way, he said.

"I'll be polite and take a bite, but then I spit it out when nobody's looking and hide it under the mashed potatoes or something," he said.

His unique eating habits are probably as well known as his football accomplishments, of which there are many. He blocked 10 field goals and extra points during the 1956 season—believed to be the most in league history.

St. Clair also lost five teeth when he blocked a punt against the Los Angeles Rams that season. He and Leo Nomellini performed a line stunt so well that St. Clair came through untouched and slapped the ball as Rams punter Norm Van Brocklin released it.

"There wasn't a ball for him to kick, so he kicked my face instead," St. Clair said. "They put cotton in my mouth, and I played the rest of the game."

St. Clair played both ways throughout his career. He was a dominating right tackle on offense, and played defensive line when the opposition got inside the 49ers' 20-yard line.

St. Clair was perhaps the biggest catalyst during the team's 1957 season that resulted in the 49ers' first NFL postseason appearance. He missed seven games in the middle of the season with a shoulder injury that was expected to keep him out the remainder of the year.

During his hospital stay, he wrote a note for the nurses as a constant reminder of his hearty appetite during meal times: "Large portions, please!"

The 49ers lost three consecutive games with him out of action and were seven-point underdogs against the New York Giants when St. Clair surprised his teammates at the meal the evening before the game at Yankee Stadium.

"I busted into the room and said, 'Moses has returned! I've been gone 40 days and 40 nights, and I'm here to lead you to the Promised Land,'" St. Clair said.

The 49ers defeated the Giants 27-17 the next day to start a three-game win streak that assured the team a spot in the playoffs. He received the game ball in the victorious locker room.

St. Clair was named to the Pro Bowl five times and earned all-NFL honors three times in his 11-year career. Despite so many Hall of Fame players on one team, St. Clair said it is easy to analyze why the 49ers never won a championship during that era.

"The injury factor," he said. "In those days, they didn't have the number of players that they have now. Once key players got hurt, it was difficult to replace them. In 1957, all our defensive backs got hurt. We had to put offensive backs in there against the Detroit Lions [in their playoff game]. We were ahead by 20 points in the second half, but all our backs went down."

Despite the disappointment of never winning a title, St. Clair said he got everything out of his career that he could have imagined. In 1952 he transferred to Tulsa after USF's football team disbanded after its legendary undefeated 1951 season.

Pete Rozelle, who was athletic publicity director at USF, had become the Rams' general manager. (He would later become NFL commissioner.)

"He came out there to call on me," St. Clair said. "He said, 'Don't worry, you're coming back to the coast. The Rams are going to draft you in the third round.'"

Instead, the 49ers grabbed him in the third round with the No. 27 overall selection.

"That was when there were only 12 teams in the league, so I would've been a first-rounder today," he said.

During a time when players often worked other jobs in the offseason to supplement their incomes, St. Clair moonlighted as the elected mayor of Daly City, the town just south of San Francisco. He served in that role from 1958 to 1964. He was on the San Mateo County Board of Supervisors from 1966 to 1974.

His political career came to an end after losing elections in the mid-1970s for the State Senate and the San Francisco Board of Supervisors. In the supervisor race, he lost to Harvey Milk, who was assassinated in 1978, along with San Francisco Mayor George Moscone.

St. Clair moved to Santa Rosa, more than 50 miles north of San Francisco, around 1980 to work as a manager for a chain of liquor stores. He still lives there but now works for Clover dairy products.

"I'm sales, public relations ... I do everything but milk the cow," he said.

St. Clair has been married to his second wife, Marsha, for more than 20 years. He has six sons and daughters, 16 grandchildren and seven great grandchildren. He also takes part in about a dozen memorabilia shows a year, he said. St. Clair can be found every NFL preseason in Canton, Ohio, where he proudly attends the annual Hall of Fame weekend.

"I've been back to the Hall of Fame induction ceremony every year since I got in," he said. "I like to support the new guys coming in, because I know how much it means to me."

R.C. "ALLEY OOP" OWENS

Under the cover of darkness and hiding among strangers, R.C. Owens did the same thing in city after city during the months of the football season.

As the alumni coordinator for the 49ers, he made every road trip with the team. He was diagnosed with hypertension in 1994, and two years later he began undergoing dialysis treatments for a kidney ailment three times a week.

Every Tuesday, Thursday and Saturday, Owens would make sure he was in the dialysis chair at 4:30 a.m. Because the 49ers travel for most road games on Fridays, Owens would have to find dialysis centers in different cities across America.

When the schedule came out in the spring, he would start making arrangements in such cities as Philadelphia, Atlanta and Green Bay, Wisconsin. He typically left the team hotel in the wee hours for his three-hour, 45-minute treatments so nobody would see him leaving or coming back.

Owens secretly waited for a kidney transplant, not wanting those with the organization to be worried with the intimate details of his life.

"It was one of those things where I just wanted to shut out the outside world," Owens said. "I didn't want a lot of people knowing what was happening to me and feeling sorry for me."

Through it all, Owens remained as upbeat as ever, a smile permanently painted on his face and his spirit indefatigable.

Finally, when Owens received his kidney transplant on July 4, 2004, it was all right to let his friends and admirers in on a secret he had kept hidden from all but his closest loved ones.

"This is the right time for everybody to find out," he said.

The road to his kidney transplant was a painful one. In 1996, he received a phone call telling him they had found a match. However, his mother had died three days earlier and Owens was going to San Diego to deliver the eulogy.

After passing up that opportunity, Owens began to wonder when he might get another chance to receive a kidney. It wasn't until he was speaking with an acquaintance in the medical field that he found out the truth.

Owens told the person he was on the transplant list. A couple days later, the friend called to tell him the bad news. For some reason, Owens was no longer on the recipient list.

He spoke with administrators at the hospital who told him he had been removed from the list after they failed to track him down after he moved from the Bay Area city of Danville to Manteca, less than an hour's drive east.

R.C. "ALLEY OOP" OWENS

Flanker · College of Idaho · Ht. 6-3; Wt. 197
Born: November 12, 1934 · 49ers career: 1957-1961

Career highlights: Selected in 14th round of 1956 draft · Led 49ers in receiving in 1960 with 55 catches for 1,032 yards and five TDs · Led team in 1960 with six TD receptions · Played 89 games in eight-year NFL career · Also played for Baltimore Colts (1962 and 1963) and New York Giants (1964) · Caught 206 passes for 3,285 yards and 22 TDs in career.

Three days after that meeting, Owens received another call telling him the good news: He was back on the list and in his original spot. About two months later, Owens got a 6 a.m. call on July 4, telling him to be at the hospital by 10 a.m. He and his wife made it there at 9:40 a.m.

By 10 p.m. that evening, Owens had his new kidney and a new outlook on life. "I'm developing a whole new lifestyle," said Owens, who no longer has to worry about upholding a strict diet.

R.C. Owens is one of the most celebrated players in 49ers history. He still answers to the nickname, "Alley-Oop," for the athletic feat that has become a widely used description of one of basketball's most exciting plays.

Owens, who played five seasons for the 49ers after being a 14th-round draft pick out of the College of Idaho in 1956, became famous for his leaping catches of passes lofted far downfield. Quarterback Y.A. Tittle knew all he had to do was throw the ball in the air above the defenders, and there was a good chance Owens would use his six-foot-three frame to catch the pass before anybody else could get a finger on it.

In Owens's rookie season, the "Alley-Oop" became a staple of the 49ers' success. The play made its debut October 6, 1957, against the Los Angeles Rams. Owens caught two touchdown passes in the 49ers' 23-20 victory.

"Two of the most dumbfounding, astonishing, impossible catches ever wrought on any gridiron, both by rookie halfback R.C. Owens, enabled San Francisco's 49ers to walk out of this jungle proud victors," wrote Bill Leiser of the *San Francisco Chronicle*.

Owens made a leaping 12-yard touchdown catch over Rams cornerback Jesse Castete in the back corner of the end zone in the closing seconds to provide the winning points. In the second quarter, Owens made a sensational catch of Tittle's 46-yard pass, coming down with the ball despite the tight defense of Don Burroughs and Will Sherman.

The headline in the newspaper screamed, "'Yah-HOOs!' and 'Alley-Oops!' Follow 49er Victory." The story quotes 49ers assistant coach Mark Duncan explaining that "alley-oop" is the name given to the play.

"He goes up in the air like a tight-coiled spring, and he holds onto that ball," Duncan said of Owens.

The next week, Owens made another alley-oop catch against the Chicago Bears, but the winning score came when he caught a touchdown pass on his knees. Owens had fallen down in the end zone but managed to latch onto Tittle's pass with 27 seconds left for a 21-17 victory.

Never was the alley-oop used at a more dramatic time than during a midseason game against the Detroit Lions. The 49ers, trailing 31-28, held the ball at the Lions' 42-yard line in the final seconds.

Everybody knew what was coming, but the Lions still could not stop it. All-Pro Jack Christiansen and Jim David tried to cover Owens, but Owens went high into the air to grab Tittle's pass in the end zone for a remarkable 35-31 victory at Kezar Stadium.

Owens caught five touchdown passes his rookie season. He also caught the team's first touchdown in an NFL playoff game, grabbing Tittle's 34-yard alley-oop pass in the first quarter for a 7-0 lead against the Lions. The 49ers led 24-7 at halftime, but Detroit rallied for a 31-27 victory.

In Owens's final season with the 49ers in 1961, he led the team with 55 catches for 1,032 yards and five touchdowns, as John Brodie had now taken over full time for Tittle.

Owens went to the Baltimore Colts in 1962, where he again created excitement with his extraordinary athletic skills. In a game against the Was-hington Redskins, Owens lined up under the goal post for Bob Khayat's 40-yard field-goal attempt.

In those days, the goal posts were on the goal line. When the line-drive kick was about to clear the crossbar, Owens jumped in the air and swatted the ball away, like a basketball player blocking a shot. Not coincidentally, Owens was also a standout basketball player in college.

Two years later, the NFL made the play illegal. Now a field-goal attempt can only be blocked at the line of scrimmage.

Owens finished his career with two seasons in Baltimore and one year with the New York Giants. But he rejoined

R.C. Owens, who helped keep the history of the organization alive, still regularly attends 49ers home games.
Photo courtesy of Dan Audick

the 49ers organization in 1979 when newly hired head coach Bill Walsh needed a liaison to help rebuild the bridge to the team's former players. Owens filled the role as the alumni coordinator for the next 24 years, where his impact on the organization was immeasurable.

"R.C. pioneered it," said Keena Turner, who along with Eric Wright, Jesse Sapolu, Guy McIntyre and Steve Bono, has taken over the alumni responsibilities. "It took five of us to fill his shoes."

JERRY MERTENS

Jerry Mertens knew it was going to be tough to make the 49ers after he was selected in the 20th round of the 1958 draft out of Drake University.

He was drafted as an end or wide receiver, but he made sure to be signed to a double contract, he said. If Mertens wasn't going to make the team as an end, he wanted an opportunity to try out at cornerback.

"After a week and a half of rookie camp, I knew I wasn't going to make it," Mertens said. "They allowed me to hang out with the veterans and try out at cornerback."

In the meantime, Mertens had an opportunity to become a high school teacher and coach at a high school close to where the 49ers had training camp at St. Mary's College in Moraga, California.

"The superintendent gave me an ultimatum," Mertens said. "He said he wanted to know the Friday before Labor Day whether I was going to take the job."

That left Mertens in a bit of a dilemma. So he paid a visit to 49ers head coach Frankie Albert.

"I was trying to put it all together as a rookie, and what I really wanted him to say was that I made the team," Mertens said. "But it came out that I had a wife and two kids in Des Moines, Iowa, and I was somewhat in debt."

Albert asked, "How much money do you want?"

"I didn't know what to say," Mertens said. "I wish I hadn't said it, but I said, $2,500."

Albert saw to it that Mertens received an advance of $2,500 on his $6,500 salary. Mertens then called the superintendent and thanked him for the opportunity.

"I'm playing pro football," Mertens said.

It was going to be difficult for Mertens to see any time on offense with such receivers as Billy Wilson, R.C. Owens and Clyde Connor already on the team. But within a week, Mertens was the starting left cornerback.

A few months later, Mertens joined teammates Hugh McElhenny, Leo Nomellini, Bob St. Clair and Wilson at the Pro Bowl.

As a rookie, Mertens drew the unenviable assignment of covering future Hall of Famer Lenny Moore when the 49ers twice played the Baltimore Colts. Mertens shut down Moore in both of those games. So when Baltimore coach Weeb Ewbank was looking for a cornerback to fill out his roster for the all-star game, he asked the 49ers to send Mertens to Los Angeles, where the game was held.

JERRY MERTENS

Defensive back · Drake University · Ht. 6-0; Wt. 184
Born: January 5, 1936 · 49ers career: 1958-1965

Career highlights: Selected in 20th round of 1958 draft ·
Converted from end to defensive back as rookie · Named to
Pro Bowl team in 1958 · Returned an interception 30 yards for
a touchdown in 1958 · Recorded six career interceptions ·
Played 91 games in seven seasons, all with the 49ers.

"The whole thing was pretty exciting," Mertens said. "I would've played the game for nothing. It was pretty exciting to make the team, and I thank God that I had enough talent that I could play for a while. Just playing for the 49ers was my dream when I got drafted."

Mertens played eight seasons with the 49ers, but his career came to an abrupt end the final game of the 1965 season.

Mertens came up from his left cornerback position to deliver a big hit on Green Bay Packers fullback Jim Taylor for a six-yard loss. But Mertens immediately knew something was wrong.

He needed smelling salts on the field but was able to get up and walk off the field. He sat on the bench but could not move his head. He went to the hospital for X-rays, but the doctors could not find anything wrong with him. Mertens even went to the team party that night.

But the next morning, Mertens could not raise his head off the pillow. His wife drove him to the hospital, and he did not leave for three months.

Mertens had sustained multiple fractures to the atlas, which is the first of seven cervical vertebrae. The atlas bears all the weight of the skull, and Mertens would soon find out he was just lucky to be alive.

"Any time you break the atlas vertebra, it's usually fatal," Mertens said. "Thank God it stayed together."

Initially, there was talk of fusing the atlas and axis vertebrae, but Mertens' orthopedic doctor advised waiting to see if the atlas would heal on its own. Holes were drilled in his head for stabilization and eventually he was enclosed in a 55-pound body cast. It took him a year before he could get back on his feet.

He spent the 1966 season on injured reserve and never stepped on the playing field again.

"I didn't want to give up playing football, but it helped knowing that the doctors were right," Mertens said. "It made it easier to accept being out of the game."

Mertens said there are times when he still feels discomfort in that region of his neck. "I have other things, too, like bad knees, bad shoulders, and a bad back," he said. "That's the price you pay for playing the game."

Mertens worked for Balfour-Guthrie, an importer-exporter, in the offseasons while he played for the 49ers. He sold a lot of chemical fertilizer and later went into that line of work with his own company. He finally got completely out of the business in 2003.

Since the 1970s, he's been involved with NFL Alumni, Inc., a charitable organization that supports activities for children. Their annual golf tournament at San Francisco's prestigious Olympic Club raises close to $100,000 for youth programs. He has been the president of the Northern California chapter of the NFL Alumni for more than seven years.

Mertens lives in the Bay Area and continues to be a loyal supporter of the 49ers, with his 20 season tickets as evidence.

"I'd bring customers and friends to games at Kezar and Candlestick," Mertens said. "There is always a good following of people who would want to come out. [But in 2004], it was disastrous. It got to the point where I couldn't even give the tickets away."

CHARLIE KRUEGER

Charlie Krueger likes to go fishing, work in his yard and read books that dispense lessons in life. He lists Leo Tolstoy and James Conrad among his favorite authors.

"I try to read something that's worthwhile," said Krueger, who has been retired since selling his liquor store in the early 1990s. "I want something that teaches me or shows me. I want to find something in what I'm reading. That's just the nature in man."

Krueger was a rough-and-tumble defensive tackle who played for the 49ers from 1959 to 1973, wearing his trademark two-bar facemask. One year after he stopped playing, the 49ers retired his No. 70 jersey.

But that is all he left behind from his playing days, he says.

"Football is a hell of a way to live," said Krueger, who lives in the Bay Area community of Clayton, California, near Mt. Diablo. "It just happened that way for me. When I got out of high school, the easiest thing for me to continue on in school was to accept a scholarship. I wasn't that highly sought after. I received three offers, so I went to school."

Krueger enrolled at Texas A&M in 1954, and was lucky enough he did not have to go with coach Paul "Bear" Bryant to the legendary 10-day training camp in Junction, Texas. Only 35 of the 111 players who began the camp came back to campus as members of the team.

"He ran off more good players from A&M than he kept," Krueger said. "He paid for it. They went 1-9 that year. I'm glad freshmen couldn't participate."

Krueger made it through all four seasons at A&M, including the team's 9-0-1 turn-around two years later that included a Southwest Conference championship. The Aggies were ineligible for the Cotton Bowl, however, because of a two-year ban for NCAA rules violations. Krueger said he remained at A&M only because he did not have the courage to quit the team.

"If you quit, you're no f——ing good—you're a quitter, you're yellow," he said. "You'd wonder, 'Why am I doing this? Am I f——ing nuts?' I came back one day and my roommate was gone. I admired his guts."

Krueger became a first-round draft pick of the 49ers in 1958, and he found professional football much more to his liking—sort of.

"It was a lot easier, but football is football," Krueger said. "The nature of football is cold. That's just the way it has to be. I was young, and I see things differently now. My hearing is not as good, but I listen better. My eyes might not be as good, but I see better."

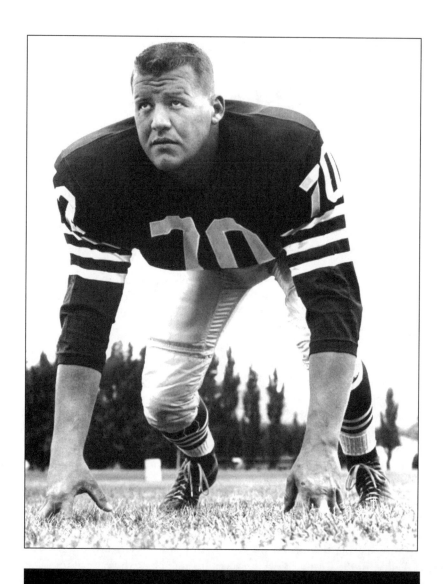

CHARLIE KRUEGER
Defensive lineman · Texas A&M · Ht. 6-4; Wt. 256
Born: January 28, 1937 · 49ers career: 1959-1973

Career highlights: First-round draft pick in 1958 · Named to Pro Bowl team in 1960 and 1964) · Second-team All-NFL in 1960 and 1965 · Honorable-mention All-NFL in 1966 · Len Eshmont Award winner in 1964 · Jersey No. 70 retired in 1974.

While Krueger was playing, he was known for his passion. There certainly weren't any hints he would rather be doing something else.

"How can I describe Charlie? Very, very, very intense," longtime teammate Len Rohde said. "Back then, he was in love with it—or in love with some part of it. Whatever Charlie did, he did with 110-percent intensity."

Rohde recalls the 49ers would have their pregame meal at 8 a.m. While most of the players would arrive at the stadium at 10:30 or 11 a.m. for a 1 p.m. game, Krueger would be one of a handful of players to leave for the stadium straight from breakfast.

But Krueger has reason to view the sport differently now. Nearly four years after his retirement, he realized he sustained permanent damage to his knee while playing through injuries with the help of painkillers and steroids for medicinal purposes.

The 49ers were found liable for fraudulent concealment after failing to inform him of the risks of continuing to play with the injuries. A judge initially ruled in Krueger's favor, issuing a tentative order for the 49ers to pay $2.36 million, but a reported settlement of approximately $1 million was reached in 1992.

"That was strictly business," Krueger said. "I understand that happens in business and happens with companies other than football companies. I went to court, and nine judges out of 10 agreed with me."

Krueger, of course, still feels the effects from his football days. He has arthritis, so he has to remain active.

"I have to work out every day," he said. "I either work out with weights or go for a walk. If you don't stay active, you lose the range of motion or muscle, and you slowly start giving it away. Anyway, I miss football like a f—-ing car wreck."

Although Krueger said he does not enjoy watching football, he has been welcomed back into the 49ers family. He attends the 49ers' alumni functions whenever he gets a chance. In October 2004, Krueger went to his 50th high school reunion, which fell the same time as the 49ers alumni weekend. He made sure to inform 49ers owner John York that he would not be able to make it.

"They call us the alumni, I call us the crips and gimps," Krueger said. "They have treated us well, though. I didn't want the Yorks to think I was turning a shoulder to their kind offer."

Krueger is pleased the 49ers have turned back the clock with the selection of Mike Nolan as head coach. Mike Nolan was nine years old when his father, Dick, took over as coach of the 49ers in 1968.

"Dick Nolan was a very serious man, and I never did see a harder working man than him," Krueger said. "He is a very decent man, and I know his family is all the same way. I wish Mike Nolan well. He's a fine fellow. I hope the situation works out, because there are so many variables."

Krueger, known during his playing days as one of the great pranksters, hit if off very well with the kid who would become coach of the 49ers. During his introductory press conference, Mike Nolan recounted how he worked as Krueger's accomplice.

Backup quarterback George Mira was known for arriving in the locker room just in the nick of time to get dressed and make it onto the practice field. One day, Krueger grabbed Mira's practice jersey and pads out of his locker. He instructed Mike Nolan to climb onto his shoulders. He handed Mira's gear to the kid and then gave him white athletic tape to fasten the apparel to a white pole in the locker room.

"He said, 'Take that tape,' and we proceeded to walk about 100 times around that pole until it was white-on-white and you couldn't see his uniform," Nolan said.

Mira couldn't find his practice clothes, so he had to grab someone else's pads and jersey, Nolan said. He was late getting to practice, so Dick Nolan fined him.

"Even though George told him what happened, my dad stood by his son," Mike Nolan said.

MONTY STICKLES

M onty Stickles, perhaps more than any player in 49ers' history, experienced the city of San Francisco during and after his playing days.

He was born in Chicago, but he believes he lived more years in The City than any other player in 49ers history. He spent 40 years, from 1962 to 2002, with a residence in San Francisco before moving across the bay to Alameda.

Stickles, a fun-loving and colorful character, certainly enjoyed his time as a bachelor on the prowl in one of the most vibrant cities in America.

"Billy Kilmer and Lou Cordileone, at different times we roomed together," Stickles said. "It was the 1960s, and the women were on the pill, and there were no AIDS or herpes. The women were really nice and they dressed a lot better than they do now. We had a lot of fun, three bachelor guys on the town every night in San Francisco."

Stickles did plenty of scoring on the field, too.

A No. 1 draft pick from Notre Dame, the tight end caught 14 touchdown passes in his eight seasons with the team. His best season was 1961 when had 43 receptions for 794 yards and five touchdowns.

Stickles was part of one of the better receiving corps in the league for a period of time, teaming with split end Dave Parks and flanker Bernie Casey.

A player who was never shy about dishing out some punishment to unsuspecting defenders, Stickles said the wildest thing he ever did on the field involved a cheap shot that helped the 49ers avoid a loss in 1966.

The 49ers had the ball on their own 17-yard line with 40 seconds remaining, trailing the Chicago Bears 30-27 at Wrigley Field. On a fourth-and 23, quarterback John Brodie found Casey for a 29-yard completion.

But something else was going on away from the play.

"I elbowed a guy in the back of the head as the game was ending," Stickles admitted. "I didn't get caught, and then he started kicking me as I walked away. He got flagged for unsportsmanlike conduct."

It really happened. Bears linebacker Joe Fortunato's penalty put 49ers kicker Tommy Davis in position for a 44-yard field goal with nine seconds remaining to enable the 49ers to salvage a 30-30 tie.

"He's the dirtiest player in the NFL," Fortunato said of Stickles afterward. "He could have broken my neck. One of these days, he's going to pay for it."

Stickles never did.

MONTY
STICKLES
S. F. 49'ERS
END

The Topps Company, Inc.

MONTY STICKLES
End · Notre Dame · Ht. 6-4; Wt. 232
Born: August 16, 1938 · 49ers career: 1960-1967

Career highlights: Selected in first round of 1960 draft · Tied
for team lead with five TD catches in 1961 · Caught 222 passes for 3,199 yards and 16 touchdowns in career · Played 115
games in nine-year NFL career · Also played for
New Orleans Saints in 1968.

He had a lot of fun on and off the field. Stickles said he generally controlled the amount of partying he sought the night before games. But there was one time he admittedly had a few too many drinks.

The night before the 49ers' 1963 trip to Baltimore, Stickles visited the hotel of his parents, who had traveled down from Poughkeepsie, New York, to watch the game.

"It was the first time I ever drank with my dad," Stickles said. "He went to bed, and I stayed up talking to my mom. I didn't get to bed until four in the morning. I wasn't even hung over yet when the game started. I dropped a couple balls, and they took me out of the game. That was the only time I got into trouble like that."

After his career, Stickles entered the radio industry. After three years at KEST, a small station in San Francisco, he landed a job at powerful KGO in 1972. While at KGO, he was the first person in the Bay Area market to try a different format called sports talk.

"I was the guy who got it started," Stickles said.

He engaged in an hour show, from 6 to 7 p.m., five nights a week. The popular show was soon expanded to two hours. He also did sports reports during drive time.

The most memorable moment of Stickles's radio career happened in 1984 when he got into a rather animated shouting match with former San Francisco Giants manager Frank Robinson in his office.

"Frank went f——ing crazy," Stickles said. "We had to bleep him 23 times in 56 seconds."

Robinson had brought relief pitcher Gary Lavelle into the game after he had been out of action with a knee injury. Lavelle got roughed up in his short stint. So Robinson was already seething when the question was asked, "Do you think you brought Lavelle back too soon?"

The quick-tempered Robinson attempted to dismiss the question as bogus when Stickles interjected that the question was legitimate. He and Robinson went nose to nose in a classic, obscenity-filled confrontation that quickly became legendary.

"That's a horseshit question," Robinson said. "I'm f——ing telling you, if he wasn't f——ing healthy he wouldn't be out there."

After a little more heated dialogue, Robinson ordered Stickles out of his office but noticed he was still recording the events.

"He starts swatting at my mike, and I keep moving it so he can't hit it," Stickles said. "Later I thought, 'Here's one of the greatest hitters of all time, and he couldn't even make contact with my mike.'"

The Giants went on a road trip after that game, and Stickles had to deal with Robinson only one more time. Robinson was fired after his team stumbled to a 42-64 record through two-thirds of the season.

A year later, Stickles got out of the radio business and began selling beer for a Bay Area distributor. Labatt's hired him to cover the entire Bay Area. After 20 years, he retired from his job in September 2004. But he was already contemplating getting back in the business after refurbishing a Victorian house he recently bought in downtown San Jose.

BERNIE CASEY

B ernie Casey might have been the most talented individual who ever played for the 49ers. He was an upper-echelon wide receiver, but he also had an abundance of talent—and passion—in the arts.

Not only was he a three-time honorable-mention All-Pro flanker, who led the team in receiving three straight seasons in the 1960s, he left football after eight seasons to concentrate on acting and painting.

Casey spent more than 20 years as chair of the board of trustees at the prestigious Savannah College of Art and Design, the largest school of its kind in America. But he is also an acclaimed artist and a thriving Hollywood actor.

"He had so many talents he didn't have to rely on sports as his No. 1," said R.C. Owens, whose position Casey filled capably with the 49ers.

Casey was a first-round draft pick of the 49ers in 1961 from Bowling Green University. He led the 49ers in receiving from 1962 to 1964, with 158 catches for 2,389 yards and 17 touchdowns during that period. He caught eight touchdown passes in 1965 but ranked behind Dave Parks for the team lead in receptions.

After Casey was traded at the beginning of the 1967 season, he spent his final two years in the league with the Los Angeles Rams. He pursued his other interests full time after leaving the NFL with 359 catches for 5,444 yards and 40 touchdowns during his eight-year career.

Casey declined to be interviewed for this project, sending word through a friend that his football career was a lifetime ago and he had no desire to revisit it. He does not keep in contact with many of his former teammates, some of whom described him as a "loner." However, former 49ers running back David Kopay said he considers Casey "a wonderful guy and a very close friend."

"Bernie was very composed; he had his shit together, so to speak," ex-49ers teammate Len Rohde said. "He always looked good. He had good clothes and a good hairdo."

Niners teammate Monty Stickles said Casey got him interested in art more than 40 years ago. Stickles attended Casey's first art exhibit, which took place in San Francisco's John Bolles Gallery in 1963.

"I went to support a teammate," Stickles said. "I have a couple of his paintings in my collection. His works are non-objective. He lays down some nice colors and composition."

BERNIE CASEY
Flanker · Bowling Green · Ht. 6-4; Wt. 213
Born: June 8, 1939 · 49ers career: 1961-1966

Career highlights: First-round selection in 1961 · Led 49ers in receiving in 1962, 1963 and 1964 · All-NFL honorable mention in 1965 and 1966 · Caught 359 passes for 5,444 and 40 touchdowns in career · Played 105 games in eight-year career · Finished career with Los Angeles Rams in 1967 and 1968.

Stickles is not alone in his appreciation of Casey's art. Dr. Maya Angelou, Sidney Poitier, Burt Reynolds, Jim Brown, and Bill Russell reportedly own some of Casey's work.

In a press release to promote Casey's 2003 exhibit at the Thelma Harris Art Gallery in Oakland, Angelou explains her fascination with Casey's work.

"I cannot see what Bernie Casey sees," she said "Casey has the heart and the art to put his insight on canvas, and I am heartened by his action. For then I can comprehend his vision and even some of my own. His art makes my road less rocky, and my path less crooked."

Casey's exhibit, consisting of more than 20 works of art, was entitled, "Hopes and Dreams and Spring."

When asked about the title, Casey said, "Hope is the cornerstone of all our possibilities. It allows our dreams to come true. For no matter how unrelenting winter may seem, spring is inevitable."

Casey has had more than 30 solo exhibitions, and his works are in the permanent collections at the Hirshhorn Museum in Washington, D.C., and the California Museum of African American Art in San Francisco. In 1976, he was selected to represent the North American Zone in the second World Black and African Arts and Culture Festival held in Lagos, Nigeria.

Casey, who lives in Southern California, was the subject of an NFL Films piece in 1999, during which he told interviewer Steve Sabol he never loved the game of football.

"You don't have to love it," he said, "just be proficient at it. People do things all the time that they don't love, and they're good at it. It's a steppingstone to get from one place to another. It allows you facility to pursue much bigger, more important visions."

He said he only played in the NFL for the money.

"I was big, agile, fast and a dedicated athlete," he said. "But I always wanted to be a painter."

In another NFL Films interview from 1967, Casey said, "If I could get the money from my paintings that I get playing football, I'd tell the whole NFL to [bleep] off."

Casey said the most daunting obstacle football players must overcome is the reality they will be considered washed up at such an early age.

"When that sojourn is over and you're 32 or something, when most people are just beginning to understand who they are, what they can do and what life is all about, you have been considered in the world of sports a dinosaur," Casey told NFL Films. "From that point on, it's a downward spiral into the abyss of non-consideration and obscurity and a lot of other things that they never recover from. I want to think in my instance, it's the beginning. There's a lot of life left after 32."

And Casey has certainly experienced it.

He made his acting debut in 1969 in *The Guns of the Magnificent Seven*. His list of credits also includes: Martin Scorsese's *Boxcar Bertha*, *Cleopatra Jones*, *Brian's Song*, *Black Gun*, *Hit Man*, *Roots: The Next Generations*, *The Man Who Fell to Earth*, *Sharkey's Machine*, *Never Say Never Again*, *Under Siege*, *Another 48 Hours*, *Revenge of the Nerds*, and *Bill and Ted's Excellent Adventure*.

He's also appeared in guest roles on numerous television series, including *Murder, She Wrote*, *L.A. Law*, *Trapper John, M.D.*, and, appropriately, *The Streets of San Francisco*.

DAVID KOPAY

David Kopay was a hard-working, overachieving running back and special-teams standout who managed to stick in the NFL for a decade.

He played the first four years of his career with the 49ers as an undrafted free agent, and later played on legendary coach Vince Lombardi's final team, the 1969 Washington Redskins.

But Kopay's achievements on the football field are a mere backdrop to the impact he has made in the area of social awareness and tolerance.

In 1975, he became the first major American team athlete to publicly announce he was gay.

More than 30 years later, Kopay continues to be the unofficial spokesman whenever the subject arises in the sporting world. It is a responsibility he acknowledges has been difficult at times.

"Absolutely, I get tired of it," he said. "But my friends say, 'Shut the hell up, that's what you're here for.' I used to get angry and wonder why I always had to be put on the spot. 'Why can't I have any privacy?' But those are fleeting thoughts.

"Do I regret speaking out? I've never regretted it. That's my way of breathing and opening up and living and getting in contact with the rest of the world. The biggest negative about being a public gay figure is the lack of privacy you have in developing relationships. People are reluctant to deal with my notoriety with their friends and family."

Early in his career with the 49ers, quarterback John Brodie pinned the nickname "Psyche" on him because of his over-the-top fervor to play the game. As a player who had to fight every season to make it in the NFL, Kopay could not approach his profession in any other manner.

"I kind of developed that at the University of Washington," Kopay said. "It was a conscious effort to really be more than I was because I felt somewhat deficient inside. I had this big secret. I also had my love for a fraternity brother, and I was trying to get his approval, too."

Kopay was a co-captain on Washington's Rose Bowl team his senior season. He made the 49ers as an undrafted rookie in 1964, and led the team in rushing with 271 yards. In a loss to the Chicago Bears, Kopay rushed 20 times for 91 yards and caught four passes for 57 yards.

Still, Kopay said he had a lot of questions about himself during his time in San Francisco.

Oakland Tribune file photo

DAVID KOPAY
Running back · Washington
Born: June 28, 1942 · 49ers career: 1964-1967

Career highlights: Earned roster spot in 1964 as undrafted free agent · Led 49ers in rushing in 1964 with 271 yards on 75 carries · Played 111 games in nine-year career · Also played for Detroit Lions (1968), Washington Redskins (1969-1970), New Orleans Saints (1971) and Green Bay Packers (1972).

"I didn't know I was gay when I was with San Francisco," Kopay said. "I guess I knew, but I kept hiding it and denying it. In those days I was full of piss and vinegar. Hell, you'd make love to anything. I certainly liked the affection and physical contact. I denied to myself that I was really gay or queer, which was a real nasty word. I wasn't able to accept those labels at all."

Kopay's life changed forever on December 9, 1975, after buying a copy of that day's *Washington Star*. The headline at the top of the page read, "Homosexuals in Sports/Why Gay Athletes Have Everything to Lose."

With trembling hands, Kopay reached for the phone to call reporter Lynn Rosellini. She had written the ground-breaking series, which editor Dave Burgin assigned to her.

Kopay was prepared to come out of the closet.

Kopay says the article he read, which concealed the identity of a gay athlete, was about ex-teammate Jerry Smith, who was a star tight end for the Washington Redskins.

"Jerry and I had a deep emotional and physical love for one another and had many times discussed our dilemma," Kopay said in a 2004 graduation speech to the University of Washington's lesbian, gay, bisexual and transgender students.

"We even discussed writing a book together and telling the world the truth. We laughed and we spoke of setting the record straight, so to speak. But I knew Jerry would never

David Kopay, who kept his sexuality a secret when he played for the 49ers, shows his playful side during this promotional photo with a cheerleader.
Oakland Tribune file photo

do something like that. Not in a million years.... Jerry was a huge star, and his closet door was bolted shut."

Kopay decided to respect Smith's privacy, so he never "outed" him. Kopay said Smith could not find peace of mind with his own sexuality. Smith died of AIDS-related complications in 1986.

Kopay suggests Smith's legacy has been tarnished, because his sexual orientation became public knowledge with his death. Smith is not in the Pro Football Hall of Fame, though his statistics clearly support his case. And when Shannon Sharpe broke his NFL record for most career touchdown catches by a tight end, Smith was rarely spoken or written about as the man whose record was being broken, Kopay points out.

Two years after having his story written in the Washington Star, Kopay wrote a book, *The David Kopay Story*, along with author Perry Deane Young. The book spent ten weeks on *The New York Times* bestseller list.

Although there was predictably some negative reaction to his disclosure, Kopay said he was overwhelmed by the support he received, especially from many of his former teammates.

"I've seen Dave many times since, and I don't view him any different today than I did when we were teammates," former teammate Len Rohde said.

Former 49ers guard Howard Mudd, his roommate all four years with the team, was one of the first people Kopay confided in. Kopay was surprised with acceptance he received around the league. One time in the mid-1980s, when Mudd was coaching for the Cleveland Browns, Kopay visited him at the team hotel in Los Angeles.

"I was there with Howard, and Cody Risien, this big offensive tackle who was becoming a minister, was also there," Kopay said. "Howard introduced me to his guys. Risien had read my book. Here's a straight guy, a minister, and he complimented me on it. That was just amazing to me."

As well as he has been received from the football world, Kopay said he believes an American athlete in one of the major sports should be able to come out of the closet during his playing career without it becoming too overwhelming.

"Of course, everybody says I'm living in a dreamland," Kopay said. "But I thought it would happen by now. I spoke out in 1975. That's really a lifetime ago. It's super disappointing to me that it hasn't happened, yet. I think now that it'll happen in college ball before it happens in the pros."

Kopay owns a beautiful home and lives comfortably in Los Angeles. He had worked since 1980 for a Hollywood floor-covering company that primarily sells to the entertainment industry, providing floors to movie producers and television shows.

The rigors of football have caught up to him, as he has undergone surgeries to replace his knee, hip, and shoulder in recent years. But that has not slowed him down from carrying such a huge load as an ambassador for gay causes.

JOE CERNE

Joe Cerne is in rare company as being one of the few NFL players born in Yugoslavia who was not a kicker.

He came to the United States in 1952 at the age of nine, but has visited the area that's now Slovenia, five times since the mid-1970s after inheriting a 44-acre farm upon his mother's death in 1995. Cerne still owns the property.

Cerne is the first to admit his four-year NFL career was not spectacular, but that does not mean it was uneventful. A second-round 1965 draft pick from Northwestern, Cerne was almost the same size as first-round selection Ken Willard.

The difference is that Willard was a running back; Cerne was a center.

"When I was with the 49ers, I was small and slow," Cerne said. "I always thought, 'I have to make the team one more year.' I just didn't have the size to play on the offensive line, but I enjoyed my four years tremendously."

Although Cerne rarely got on the field with the offensive unit with the late Pro Bowl center Bruce Bosley manning the position, he was the team's long snapper for punts, field goals and extra points.

"It was a wonderful time," Cerne said. "I came in with guys like Ken Willard, and what I remember most was Monty Stickles and his antics on the field."

Cerne went to the Atlanta Falcons in 1968, and his first career was over one year later. However, his second career, which began in 1970, is still going strong.

He graduated from Northwestern University in Evanston, Illinois, with a degree in political science and international relations. "I had some chemistry classes, but not a lot," Cerne said.

He went to work for International Minerals and Chemical Company, headquartered in Skokie, Illinois, in 1969. He was sent to Des Moines, Iowa, to be their feed phosphate salesman. He launched Cerne Calcium Company in 1975.

Cerne is in the business of ground calcium carbonate, which is a raw mineral used in feed ingredients. Today, Cerne Sales Company offers "poultry and swine integrators, livestock producers and feed manufacturers with the minerals and nutrients essential to blue-ribbon animal nutrition," according to the company's web site. Cerne said they serve the animal feed industry for the production of meat, milk and eggs.

Their high-grade calcium carbonate is also used for the glass industry, Cerne said.

"We're not a large company, but it is ours," said Cerne. "I have less than 20 employees. We've just been plugging along, and we've been successful every year."

JOE CERNE
Center · Northwestern · Ht. 6-2; Wt. 238
Born: April 26, 1942 · 49ers career: 1965-1967

Career highlights: Second-round selection in 1965 · Was team's
long-snapper on field goals and punts · Played 45 games in
four seasons · Finished career with Atlanta Falcons
in 1968 · Wore number 56.

DAVE PARKS

Several years after their playing careers were over, John Brodie finally let Dave Parks know how he felt.

Brodie was still mad at Parks for leaving the 49ers during what should have been the prime of his career. Parks, as it turns out, also regrets the decision he made that brought his 49ers days to an end after the 1967 season.

"It was a bad move," Parks said. "I had a great offensive line and a great quarterback. As a receiver, you're nothing without a quarterback who has time to throw the ball.

"The thing is, I really missed those guys. I know why John was upset with me. When [head coach] Dick Nolan took over, he straightened out the defense, which was our weakness. I always felt there was something bothering John—something just wasn't right. After I left the team, we continued to socialize. He finally let me know that, in his opinion, I cost him a championship."

Parks certainly will not go so far as to say the 49ers would have won the Super Bowl had he stayed around, but there is little doubt his best chance for success was with the team the Texas Tech standout joined as the No. 1 overall pick in the 1964 draft.

Two years earlier, the 49ers had selected Lance Alworth in the first round of the NFL draft, but the future Hall of Famer got away when the San Diego Chargers of the American Football League signed him. This time, the 49ers were determined to win the bidding contest over the Chargers and the Calgary Stampeders of the Canadian Football League.

"I told all of them that I wanted the best money deal," said Parks, the last No. 1 overall pick of the 49ers before the club selected quarterback Alex Smith of Utah in 2005.

Parks lived up to the hype in his first three seasons with the 49ers, as he established himself as one of the game's top pass catchers. He made the Pro Bowl his first three seasons.

In just his sixth game with the 49ers, Parks had an 83-yard touchdown catch from Brodie against the Los Angeles Rams. The next week, he hauled in an 80-yard scoring pass against the Minnesota Vikings. Two weeks later, he caught a 79-yard touchdown at Minnesota. Those plays rank Nos. 1, 2 and 3 on the 49ers' list of longest receptions by a rookie.

Parks caught 36 passes for 703 yards and eight touchdowns as a rookie. In 1965, he led the NFL with 80 receptions for 1,344 yards and 12 touchdowns. In a 27-24 loss to

DAVE PARKS
End · Texas Tech · Ht. 6-2; Wt. 202
Born: December 25, 1941 · 49ers career: 1964-1967

**Career highlights: First overall pick in 1964 draft · First-team
All-NFL in 1965, 1966 · Led league with 80 catches for 1,344
yards and 12 touchdowns in 1965 · Played 118 games in 10
seasons · Also played for New Orleans Saints (1968-1972)
and Houston Oilers (1973).**

the Baltimore Colts, Parks had 231 yards receiving, a team record that stood 20 years before Jerry Rice broke it.

"Defenses tried a lot of single coverage my first year, and I had pretty good success against that," Parks said. "The next year, they wouldn't let us get deep, so I ate it up underneath."

In his third season, Parks caught 66 passes for 974 yards and five touchdowns, and appeared to be well on his way to making an indelible mark on the game as one of the most explosive receivers in history.

"He was a fabulous receiver, maybe the best I ever played with," 49ers teammate Ken Willard said. "If things had gone differently, he might be in the Hall of Fame."

His fourth season with the 49ers began poorly, as he held out for about a week of training camp in hopes of gaining a long-term contract from team president Lou Spadia. His contract problems carried over to the field, where he caught just 26 passes for 313 yards.

Parks signed an original three-year contract with an option year with the 49ers. After the first three years, which would turn out to be the best three seasons of his career, he wanted more security and thought he earned it.

"They called and wanted me to stay in California, so I waited the whole summer and offseason, and they kept saying they were trying to get it all lined up," Parks said. "I didn't want to play out my option. I gave them a week to think about it, and I told them that either I was getting a contract when I came back, or I was playing out my option.

"I didn't want to talk contract during the season. I was upset because I played my butt off for three years and they were pulling that crap. I was hard-headed. I told them there'd be no negotiations during the year, and then I was gone. They didn't believe me."

Unfortunately for Parks and the 49ers, he kept his word. He played the final year of his contract and was shipped to New Orleans for the 1968 season. The Saints surrendered a first-round pick, defensive end Kevin Hardy, and a No. 1 pick in the 1968 draft for the right to sign Parks away from the 49ers.

"It didn't take me long to figure out that I would not be surrounded with the same type of talent," Parks said.

Quarterback Billy Kilmer, who had gone to the Saints from the 49ers one year earlier, struggled in his new environment, too. The Saints won just 17 games in Parks's five seasons with the club, and he never clicked with Kilmer or head coach Tom Fears.

"I just wasn't in the game plan," Parks said. "You can't do stuff if you don't get a chance. I'm not blaming anyone. John [Brodie] told me, 'Don't go where you don't have a thrower, because you'll be wasted.' I knew Kilmer was there, and I knew he could play, but there was a big difference between a passer like John Brodie and someone else.

"I was blocking, running patterns and getting open—doing the same things I did in San Francisco—except the ball wasn't coming my way."

After five disappointing seasons with the Saints, during which time he was moved to tight end, Parks played five games in 1973 with the Houston Oilers, catching just three passes for 31 yards and a touchdown.

He talked to George Allen with the Washington Redskins and Don Shula with the Miami Dolphins but both backed off after initially showing interest in signing him for the 1974 season, Parks said.

Then, in a bit of a surprise, he received a call from Fears to play for the Southern California Sun of the World Football League. Parks wanted to know something: "I don't like you, and you don't like me, so why would you want me to play for you?"

Fears told him, "Because I have a talented team, and I need a veteran who can help them out."

"I told Tom to his face, 'You're a bigger man that me.' If I'd needed something from him, I never would've called."

Parks said he had a very enjoyable season in the soon-to-be defunct league. He thought he might get another chance to play in the NFL, but his career was over at the age of 33.

Parks gave coaching a try, as he spent about six weeks with George Allen coaching tight ends for the Chicago Fire of the USFL. But he had promised his father-in-law he would go to work for him in the oil business.

Now Parks spends a lot of time doing charity work. He lives in Dallas, and has raised money for the educational fund of the Texas Rangers – the law enforcement branch, not the baseball team. He has also volunteered as a coach at football powerhouse St. Mark's School, along with former Dallas Cowboys Malcolm Walker and Mike Connelly.

He has lived in Dallas since 1973, where he lives with his wife, Susan. They have been married since 1962 and have three grown children and seven grandkids.

Where Have You Gone?

JOHN DAVID CROW

John David Crow had no idea the significance of the message his mother was about to deliver when he was home from Texas A&M during a break in his senior year.

"My mother said, 'The president of the university just called,'" Crow recalls. "He called to say I won the Heisman. I didn't know that much about it, but I figured it must be a big deal if they were bringing my parents and Carolyn [his wife] to New York for the ceremony."

Crow, the 1957 Heisman Trophy winner as college football's best player, later would become the first recipient of the prestigious honor to play for the 49ers. After beginning his career with seven seasons for the Chicago/St. Louis Cardinals, Crow came to the 49ers in a 1965 trade for cornerback/kick returner Abe Woodson.

"I tried hard, and I'm very proud and pleased with my contributions to the teams I played with," Crow said. "San Francisco was a great experience for me."

More than 30 years after he last played a football game, the honors keep coming for Crow. In February 2005, he was named the winner of the Doak Walker Legends Award. The honor, which was created by the SMU Athletic Forum, honors former outstanding running backs who also distinguished themselves as leaders in the community.

This particular achievement strikes a chord with Crow, who grew up in Springhill, Louisiana, reading about Doak Walker, the 1948 Heisman winner from Southern Methodist.

"If I had an ideal who I really looked up to, it was Doak Walker," Crow said. "I came from a little town in northwest Louisiana, and I ended up getting to know Doak and his family, and we became what I'd consider real good friends."

Walker died from injuries suffered in a ski accident in 1998. Walker was 71. The honor is special for Crow because of the man for whom the award is named.

"That was really neat," Crow said. "Here I am, almost 70 years old, and they called to say I was winning that award. It really means a lot to me."

Crow experienced a lot of success in every stage of his life. After college, he had a successful professional football career for 11 years. The Pro Football Hall of Fame selection committee named Crow as a halfback on the 1960s All-Decade Team, along with Paul Hornung, Leroy Kelly and Gale Sayers. Jim Brown and Jim Taylor were the fullbacks on that 22-player offensive team.

JOHN DAVID CROW
SAN FRANCISCO 49ERS

RUNNING BACK

The Topps Company, Inc.

JOHN DAVID CROW

Running back · Texas A&M · Ht. 6-2; Wt. 218
Born: July 8, 1935 · 49ers career: 1965-1968

Career highlights: Heisman Trophy winner in 1957 · First-round selection of Chicago Cardinals in 1958 · Still holds record for longest run in Cardinals history (83 yards) · Traded to 49ers in 1965 · Selected to Pro Bowl in first season with 49ers · Len Eshmont Award winner in 1966 · Named to NFL's All-Decade team for 1960s · Played 124 games in 11-year career.

After his playing career was over, Crow went into coaching and eventually became athletic director at his alma mater. During his time at Texas A&M, he was instrumental in bringing gender equity to the athletic program.

"I made changes in women's athletics," Crow said. "We weren't just going to do stuff for the women because Title IX told us to, we really wanted to change things and have the women's program compete."

Crow was known for his competitive nature and leadership skills. If something needed to be said in the locker room, sideline, or huddle, Crow was never shy about speaking his mind.

"He was a big influence on me," former 49ers receiver Dave Parks said. "He added a lot more class when he came into the group."

Crow earned a trip to the Pro Bowl in 1965, his first season with the 49ers, when he rushed for 514 yards and caught 28 passes for 493 yards and seven touchdowns. He and fullback Ken Willard shared most of the carries for the next three seasons.

In 1968, Crow's former teammate with the Cardinals, Dick Nolan, became head coach of the 49ers.

"He came to me after we played Oakland in the preseason and asked if I wanted to play tight end," Crow said. "I told him if he thought that would help the team get better, that's where I would play."

Crow entered that season needing just 41 yards rushing to push him over 5,000 yards for his career. He caught 31 passes for 531 yards and five touchdowns, but he added just four yards to his career rushing totals.

At one point about three-quarters of the way through the season, Crow was walking with his roommate John Brodie to a pregame meal.

He turned to Brodie and asked, "Did we just play a game yesterday?"

"No, we're playing a game today," Brodie answered.

"I knew then that it was time to hang them up," Crow said.

After that game, he informed 49ers president Lou Spadia he would be retiring at the end of the season.

Nolan, knowing Crow was closing in on the milestone of 5,000 yards, asked if he wanted to be moved back to halfback to get the necessary yardage. However, Crow declined to do something just for the record book.

"I hope that I got all of those yards trying to help the team win," Crow said. "I wanted to feel like I was helping the team, not that I was doing something for statistics."

Crow learned his football principles from coach Paul "Bear" Bryant at Texas A&M. His college career began with disappointment when he found out as a freshman at A&M he could not make the trip to Junction, Texas, for a 10-day camp.

It was probably just as well that freshmen were ineligible. The book and movie, *The Junction Boys*, was based on the events during that legendary camp.

Although Crow said a lot of the descriptions in *The Junction Boys* were exaggerated, there is no disputing that 111 players arrived at the outpost and only 35 remained after 10 days.

"It didn't depict the Coach Bryant I knew," said Crow, who would become Bryant's only Heisman winner. "He was definitely a caring and demanding person. He pushed you to your limit, but he was only doing what he felt had to be done to make you successful in life and on the field."

Crow joined Bryant's staff at Alabama as a backfield coach. Even his son, John David Jr., an all-state high-school player in Ohio, played for Bryant at Alabama.

Crow became an assistant coach with the Cleveland Browns (1972-1973) and then the San Diego Chargers' offensive coordinator (1974-1975) before becoming head coach and athletic director at Northeast Louisiana in Monroe until 1980.

After spending some time in the more lucrative business of beer distributing, Crow got back into college athletics when Texas A&M athletic director Jackie Sherrill offered him a job as associate athletic director in 1983.

In 1988 he became athletic director, a post he held until 1993 when he became a limited partner in a pari-mutuel dog track. He continued to help in fund-raising for the university until his retirement in 2001.

Crow lives on a golf course in College Station with Carolyn, with whom he celebrated a 50-year anniversary on July 2, 2004. A month later, he had both knees replaced. Six weeks and one day later, he was back on the golf course.

Crow looks back on a lot of fond memories. But all of the good that has happened in his life was tempered in 1994 when John David Jr. died in an automobile accident in Birmingham, Alabama. He left behind a wife and two daughters.

"I had a great time playing football, and I don't have any grudges or regrets," Crow said. "I got paid, but not much, to play football. I wish I could've gotten paid more, but with my wife's help, we were able to live comfortably. I wish I could've done a little more to help those people who are less fortunate than we are. And not a day goes by that we don't miss our son. But that's just the way life goes."

JOHN BRODIE

Bill Walsh taught 49ers quarterbacks such as Joe Montana and Steve Young everything they would need to know about being an NFL quarterback. But it was a 49ers quarterback—long before the quarterback guru came to the organization in 1979—who taught him.

John Brodie, who suited up 17 seasons for the 49ers, would regularly stop by the Stanford University football offices during his playing days to talk with some of the school's coaches. One of the young assistants he befriended was Walsh.

"He would take the time to sit and talk football with me," Walsh said. "I learned a lot of the mechanics, the footwork and techniques of the quarterback position from John. Later we were able to transfer those to many other quarterbacks. But I didn't have a clue about the position until I talked to John over a period of time."

Brodie is one of the greatest athletes to ever play for the 49ers. After his football career, he spent more time on his golf game. He eventually earned his spot on the Senior PGA Tour, and recorded 12 top-10 finishes in 14 years with one victory.

But the man who made his living with his athleticism and his language skills—he was also an analyst for NBC Sports for 11 years—saw his life change forever on October 23, 2000.

Brodie suffered a stroke while watching *Monday Night Football*. Doctors blamed the stroke on Brodie's smoking habit. According to his wife, Sue, the carotid artery on the left side of his neck was 100-percent blocked, and the artery on the other side was 90 percent blocked.

"First of all, he shouldn't have survived," Sue said. "It was a massive, massive stroke. He had these two young doctors who were miracle workers. They did an experimental procedure that opened up his carotid and saved his life."

In November 2004, his face displayed a constant smile and he was quick with a laugh when he was inducted into San Jose Sports Hall of Fame. His speech is getting better, but he still doesn't have use of his right arm, and he can't drive.

"I have to drive and he hates that, but that's the way it is," Sue said. "But a lot of people who have strokes can't walk because they don't have the natural gifts he has."

Obviously, things could be so much worse. In fact, Brodie's misfortune has turned into a positive in so many ways. Brodie, so near death a few years earlier, has been an inspiration to so many during his ongoing rehabilitation.

JOHN BRODIE

Quarterback · Stanford · Ht. 6-1; Wt. 198
Born: August 14, 1935 · 49ers career: 1957-1973

Career highlights: First-round selection in 1957 draft · Holds
49ers record for 17 years of service · Ranks second in team history with 31,548 yards · Named NFL MVP in 1970, throwing
for 2,941 yards with 24 touchdowns and 10 interceptions ·
Selected to Pro Bowl in 1965, 1970 · Len Eshmont Award winner in 1965 · Jersey No. 12 retired in 1973 ·
Played 200 games in his career.

"I think there's a reason he made it," Sue said. "He's influenced a lot of people who've had strokes, and he's gotten a lot of people to get checkups who wouldn't have gotten checkups. He had a blocked carotid. He could've had that taken care of, if he'd known to get a checkup."

At the recommendation of Charles Coody, a friend from the Senior Tour, Brodie traveled to Abilene, Texas, to work with some doctors and physical therapists who were running a non-traditional clinic for stroke patients. Although mainstream doctors had told him that stroke patients can't make significant improvements one year after a stroke, John proved otherwise.

Typically, Brodie would undergo rehabilitation in Texas for three weeks and then return home to the Palm Springs, California area, where a new rehab center was scheduled opened.

Its name: The John Brodie Stroke Clinic.

"It's experimental stuff that the group in Texas is bringing to California," Sue said. "There will probably be three or four around the country."

For all his success with the 49ers during his nearly two decades with the team, Brodie and his family also had to endure the scrutiny that came along with being the team's most recognizable player.

Although he was the NFL Most Valuable Player in 1970 and led the league in touchdown passes three times, including a career-high 30 in 1965, he was often the target of the jeering fans at Kezar Stadium.

According to the *San Francisco Chronicle*, Brodie once said of the volume of the boos, "I'd have heard 'em if I was down at Third and Market [streets]. I can't turn off my ears."

Sue and the kids certainly heard them. And she could react with the force of a charging linebacker.

"It used to bother the kids," Sue said. "One time I hit somebody over the head with an umbrella."

But Brodie also showed a tolerant side when it came to being the subject of the fans' wrath. He endured a particularly brutal reception in the first half of a 1961 game against the Lions that eventually ended in a 20-20 tie.

"All week long they catch hell from their bosses and maybe sometimes their wives," Brodie said. "One day a week they get out to a ballgame. All of a sudden they're the bosses—my bosses. They can shout whatever they want. They can give back what they've been getting all week."

Brodie came to the 49ers in 1957 as the No. 2 overall draft pick behind Notre Dame's Paul Hornung, whom the Green Bay Packers selected. Unlike these days when first-round draft picks routinely hold out for more money, Brodie's negotiations with owner Tony Morabito did not even hold up traffic.

Brodie met Morabito in the 49ers' offices, which were located on Market Street in downtown San Francisco. Sue, then his fiancé, waited in Brodie's double-parked car while the deal was being negotiated. The whole session lasted 10 minutes, and Brodie returned to the driver's side with a $16,000 contract.

Y.A. Tittle continued to be the 49ers' starting quarterback in Brodie's rookie season. But the pair split much of the playing duties over the course of the next three years before the 49ers dealt Tittle to the New York Giants in 1961.

Brodie ranked in the league's top 10 in passing yards 10 times during his career. He led the 49ers to three consecutive NFC playoff appearances from 1970 to 1972, losing all three to the Dallas Cowboys.

He was a constant for the 49ers through more than a few football generations. He played for four head coaches: Frankie Albert, Howard "Red" Hickey, Jack Christiansen and Dick Nolan.

Many of his former colleagues still keep in touch with him and have supported him Sue said, through the difficult times including Cedrick Hardman, Dave Parks, Bob Harrison, John David Crow, Len Rohde, Cas Banaszek, Eddie Dove, Clyde Connor, R.C. Owens, and former quarterbacks coach Jim Shofner.

"He loves them all," Sue said.

Although Brodie never won a Super Bowl, he deserves the credit of 49ers fans for the knowledge he imparted to Walsh. Through his teachings, Montana and Young, both Hall of Famers, owe Brodie a debt of gratitude. Many believe Brodie deserves a spot in the Canton, Ohio shrine, too.

Walsh said he would study Brodie on film, and what he saw was a technician and an amazing athlete who had so many different facets to his game.

"John is like the Joe Montanas or people like that who have natural instincts," Walsh said. "That's why he was so great an athlete in all the sports. He had natural competitive instincts. It's some inner sense they have that they can compete.

"What he could do is something that you don't see much any more in football, and that's put touch on his passes. He could throw the soft-screen pass; he could throw the ball deep; he could throw the ball over someone's head; and he could drill the ball, if he needed to. He was an artist in playing the game of football."

Where Have You Gone?

LEN
ROHDE

The 49ers' record book lists Len Rohde as the most durable man in team history. During the course of his 15-year career, the offensive tackle played in every regular-season game—a team-record 208 consecutive.

But what the book does not show is Rohde also played in every preseason game (89) and postseason (5) game during that time, too. And what's even more amazing, he played 302 consecutive games and to this day has not undergone any surgeries related to his career.

"I should write my secret up in a book and sell it," Rohde quipped.

And what's that secret, exactly?

"I think I probably need to thank my mom and dad," he said.

Those good genes were not always apparent. In fact, Rohde missed most of his senior football season at Palatine High School, in the farmland outside of Chicago, because of injuries to both knees.

Although Rohde was a far more successful wrestling in high school, winning the Illinois state heavyweight title as a senior, he was determined to play football in college. When none of the Big Ten Conference schools came calling, Rohde decided to go out for football at Utah State.

"I had proven myself in wrestling, and they told me that I could go out for both sports," Rohde said. "I went out for football and made it, and I quit wrestling. I decided to go skiing in the winter."

After four years at Utah State, the six foot four, 235-pound Rohde joined the 49ers in 1960 as a fifth-round draft pick. For the first three seasons of his career, he backed up and split time with Hall of Fame right tackle Bob St. Clair.

In 1964, he was switched to left tackle, where he remained until coach Dick Nolan convinced Rohde to retire after the 1975 preseason.

Rohde was always a solid player, and a reliable pass-protector for John Brodie's blindside. He had his best season in 1970, as the 49ers finished 10-3-1, won the NFC West and advanced to the NFC Championship Game.

He was selected to his only Pro Bowl after the 49ers set a league record for fewest sacks allowed in a season. The 49ers yielded just eight sacks. The record was finally beaten in 1988 when Miami's Dan Marino was sacked just seven times. Brodie was named NFL Most Valuable Player that season, as he threw for 2,990 yards with 24 touchdowns and just 10 interceptions.

LEN ROHDE

Offensive tackle · Utah State · Ht. 6-4; Wt. 246
Born: April 16, 1938 · 49ers career: 1960-1974

Career highlights: Selected in fifth round of 1950 draft · Holds
team record with 208 consecutive games played during 15-year
career · Pro Bowl in 1970 · Second-team All-NFL in 1969 ·
Honorable mention All-NFL in 1965 ·
Len Eshmont Award winner in 1974.

"As an offensive tackle, there aren't too many individual stats you can hang your hat on," Rohde said. "But I guess playing in 208 games, winning the Len Eshmont, the NFC West, going to the Pro Bowl and the sack record aren't bad."

These days, left tackles in the NFL are a hot commodity. In 2004, the average salary of the top five offensive tackles in the league was $7.42 million. That is not exactly how things worked in Rohde's days.

"No one ever called me into the office and said, 'You're a high-profile player, here's a big bonus,'" Rohde said. "That kept us from having all kinds of worries about what to do with all our money. Back then, we had to save up a few dollars, which fortunately a few of us did.

"We all had to start thinking about what we were going to do after our playing careers were over. Some people went into coaching or into business or

Len Rohde has remained in the San Francisco Bay Area and still shows unyielding support to his former team.
Photo courtesy of Dan Audick

something like that. I think it was easier for us to adjust, because we all knew we had to have careers once football was over."

The end came quite abruptly for Rohde. He was named winner of the Len Eshmont Award, which goes to the 49ers player who best exemplifies the inspiration and courage displayed by the former running back, in a 1974 vote of his teammates.

He came back for his 16th professional season and made it through the team's six-game preseason schedule.

"Dick Nolan, who was our coach, told me, 'Len, you've been a fantastic team player your whole life,'" Rohde said. "'You could probably do the team another big favor and retire.' He was probably right. My back was bothering me quite a bit, so I took the not-so-subtle hint."

More than 30 years after his retirement, Rohde's back is feeling just fine.

"I'm conscientious about doing my exercises," he said. "I'm 66, so when I get a few aches and pains, it's hard to know if it's age-related or football-related. I go out in the morning and evening and walk and ride a bike, play tennis or do some skiing."

Rohde and his wife, Beverly, were married December 17, 1961. They have one adopted son, who has four children of his own and works as a photographer in Wilmington, North Carolina.

Rohde opened his first Burger King franchise in the Bay Area in 1976. He was majority owner of six Burger Kings and five Applebee's restaurants before planning to sell most of his interest early in 2005.

"I probably wouldn't have gone to college without football," Rohde said. "I owe an awful lot to the game, and I was around people who had a great influence on me. I feel pretty grateful for the opportunities, and I wouldn't trade them for anything."

DAVE WILCOX

A mild-mannered person in nearly every aspect of his life, Dave Wilcox played football with such aggression he earned the nickname, "The Intimidator."

Wilcox made a lot of noise on the field, but he was content to remain silent as year after year passed and there was still no recognition coming from the Pro Football Hall of Fame.

Finally, after 26 years of waiting, Wilcox was enshrined at Canton, Ohio, in July 2000, entering in a class that included former 49ers Joe Montana and Ronnie Lott.

"I never really sat down and thought, 'Golly, I need to be in the Hall of Fame,'" Wilcox said.

He still might not be a member of football's most elite fraternity if it weren't for Mike Giddings, who served as the 49ers' linebackers coach from 1968 to 1973. Giddings, who runs a scouting service that evaluates NFL players, set out on a mission to get Wilcox honored after attending the induction ceremony in 1995.

"He was just special," Giddings said. "I've been in the NFL since 1968, and my job is to evaluate football players. Lawrence Taylor was a great blitzer, but I haven't seen a pure outside linebacker like Dave Wilcox."

Giddings gave Wilcox a call and told him what he had in mind. Wilcox was flattered, but he said he would not campaign for himself.

"I told him that I appreciate what he's doing, but if I don't get into the Hall of Fame, it's not the end of the world," Wilcox said. "Fortunately, Mike got the information to the right people, and they said, 'Dave does belong.' I must've done something right."

Wilcox was named All-Pro seven times during his 11-year career, and Giddings came up with some impressive statistics that could not help but sway the 36 media members who cast Hall of Fame votes.

Giddings broke down the film to come up with some amazing statistics on Wilcox, especially during the 49ers' NFC West title seasons of 1970-1972. For instance, the average run to Wilcox's side of the field went for one yard. And when the 49ers led at halftime, 95 percent of the plays in the second half of games went to the other side of the field—toward defensive end Cedrick Hardman and linebacker Skip Vanderbundt.

"The four years I was there, he went from being a pretty good player to a great player," said John David Crow, who played running back with the 49ers from 1965 to 1968. "He was always around the football. He was a long, limber guy. He didn't look strong, I

DAVE WILCOX

Linebacker · Oregon · Ht. 6-3; Wt. 235
Born: September 29, 1942 · 49ers career: 1964-1974

Career highlights: Inducted into Pro Football Hall of Fame in 2000 · Named to seven Pro Bowls and was a seven-time All-NFL selection · Recovered 12 career fumbles · Selected as winner of the Len Eshmont Award in 1967 · Played 153 games in 11-year career.

don't recall anyone going into the weight room in those days, but he had unbelievable natural strength."

Giddings pointed to one play in particular that typified Wilcox's strength. In a Monday night game against the Kansas City Chiefs in 1971, running back Wendell Hayes was trying to follow the blocks of tackle Jim Tyrer and guard Mo Moorman to Wilcox's side.

"He grabbled both of them," Giddings said. "He had one with his left hand and one with his right and threw them to the ground, and then he grabbed Hayes and made him do a cartwheel."

Said former 49ers linebacker Frank Nunley, "I'm not sure how Giddings remembers that one. Dave did something like that every game."

Fame certainly has not changed Wilcox. When a reporter came to visit his log house in Junction City, Oregon, a month prior to his induction, Wilcox proudly showed off two items in his trophy room. One was a 1971 All-Pro plaque that lists him as a cornerback. The other is a ring presented to the 49ers' all-time team with the misspelled inscription "Wilhox."

When asked how having a bust in Canton has changed him, Wilcox pauses to contemplate the question.

"Now I get to sit at the head table," he said. "When I go to a dinner or whatever function it might be, I don't have to sit in the upper deck somewhere."

Wilcox disappeared from the NFL after the 1974 season when torn cartilage in his right knee prevented him from playing at a Pro Bowl level. He returned to the quiet life in Oregon. He was a part owner in a health club and therapy center in Eugene until the early 1990s, and then he ran a lumber mill for several years.

A couple times a month, Wilcox sets off on long drives to deliver luxury motor homes to dealerships across the nation. He delights in hitting the road for journeys to as far away as Florida.

"I enjoy driving," Wilcox said. "When I was in JC [in Boise, Idaho], I drove a school bus. I was 18, and that was how I paid for my room and board."

It is not uncommon for Wilcox to drive a coach that costs as much as $800,000. Sometimes he makes the trip by himself, occasionally Merle, his wife, will join him. He does not eat, drink or sleep in the glistening new coaches.

"It's nice to get on the freeway and drive," said Wilcox, who started driving after being named to the Hall of Fame. "They're a big vehicle, and it's so much more comfortable than driving a car. I can take different routes. I've been through Texas two or three times, and I'm probably ready for another route."

Wilcox and his older brother, John, both played at Oregon. John also played the 1960 season with the NFL-champion Philadelphia Eagles, coached by Buck Shaw. Dave Wilcox's two sons, Josh and Justin, both also played at Oregon.

KEN WILLARD

You don't have to tell Ken Willard professional football has changed dramatically since his Pro Bowl days of more than 35 years ago. As a fullback, Willard led the 49ers in rushing seven consecutive seasons.

"Now fullbacks are lucky if they get 20 carries a year," he said.

And another thing …

Willard was the No. 2 overall pick in the 1965 draft, which took place November 28, 1964. His original three-year contract consisted of a $50,000 signing bonus and base salaries of $25,000 as a rookie and $27,500 both of the next two seasons.

That's a total of $130,000 for three years. Contrast that, Willard points out, with Philadelphia quarterback Donovan McNabb's blockbuster contract as the No. 2 overall pick in 1999.

"It's very simple," Willard said. "There's a $53 million difference from when I played."

Willard still ranks as the No. 3 all-time ground gainer in 49ers history. Known primarily as a short-yardage back, Willard churned out 5,930 rushing yards on 1,582 carries.

His best day in the pros was a 162-yard performance on 25 carries in the 49ers' final game of the 1968 season, a 14-12 victory over the Atlanta Falcons.

"I'm most proud of lasting in the league as long as I did," Willard said. "I missed only one game in the regular season in my nine years in San Francisco."

In fact, it was a minor miracle he missed only one game. In the 49ers' exhibition opener of the 1967 season, Willard sustained a foot injury that would not go away. Coach Jack Christiansen held him out of a game against the Colts to see if the rest would enable him to return to full strength.

However, Willard discovered after the season he had sustained a broken arch, when all during the season he thought it was just an excruciatingly painful sprain.

"I had a very tough time running on it," Willard said. "I couldn't run on it during the week. We used to shoot it up before games. If you saw my foot now, you'd understand what I'm talking about."

Playing in constant pain, Willard still managed to lead the team in rushing in 1967 with 510 yards but averaged just 3.0 yards a carry.

Willard made the Pro Bowl his first two seasons in the league. He returned for the third of his four Pro Bowl appearances in 1968 after a season in which he gained a career-high 967 and ranked second in the conference.

Ken
WILLARD
SAN FRAN. 49ERS ● RUNNING BACK

The Topps Company, Inc.

KEN WILLARD

Fullback · North Carolina · Ht. 6-2; Wt. 225
Born: July 14, 1943 · 49ers career: 1965-'73

Career highlights: First-round selection (No. 2 overall) in 1965
· Led team in rushing seven consecutive seasons (1965-1971) ·
Selected to Pro Bowl in 1966, 1968 and 1969 · Third all-time
in 49ers history with 5,930 yards rushing · Second in team
history with 1,582 carries · Played in 139 games in 10-year
career · Played final season (1974) with St. Louis Cardinals.

Known as one of the team's more fun-loving guys, Willard claims he was the target of more pranks and practical jokes than he pulled on others. He said it was not uncommon for someone such as Charlie Krueger to cut off his tie or the buttons on his shirt on the team plane.

"It was always on the trip there, so I'd have to try to get things sewn back on when we got to the hotel," Willard said.

One of the all-time great pranks was pulled on Willard when the 49ers were training at St. Mary's College in Moraga. Someone ran a garden hose into Willard's second-story room and fastened it to the head of his bed.

Early on a Saturday morning, the culprit turned on the faucet, giving Willard a refreshing wake-up call.

"That was Dave Parks," Willard said. "But nobody ever admitted to anything."

Said Parks, "That hurts. I can't believe he blamed me for that, and he didn't even try to find who really did it. That ladder outside my window didn't mean anything."

Willard looks back fondly on his playing career, though he regrets how it ended. Willard said he wishes he would not have been so territorial and had agreed to remain with the 49ers in a backup role.

Instead he went to the St. Louis Cardinals for his final season. Coincidentally, the man who remained a model of durability through his years with the 49ers returned to Candlestick Park and sustained torn knee cartilage.

Even today, Willard rues the losses to the Dallas Cowboys in the conference championship games after the 1970 and the 1971 seasons.

"Melancholy," he answered when asked how he looks back on those games.

"We should've won the first one," Willard said. "We were probably the better ball club than Dallas. By the next one in January 1972, they were the better ball club. We peaked in 1970, and for some reason we started going downhill even though we were in the playoffs for two more years."

Willard speculates the reason the 49ers did not improve after the 1970 season is because offensive coordinator Ed Hughes left to become head coach of the Houston Oilers. He took offensive line coach Ernie Zwahlen with him. The loss of those coaches severed the continuity that had been established on offense.

Willard began preparing for his life outside of football while he was still playing. He went to law school at William & Mary in 1967, and began selling life insurance. He still lives in Virginia with his wife, Bonnie, whom he married in August 1963. They have four children—all grown. He was expecting his eighth and ninth grandchildren in July 2005.

"I enjoyed my time in football, but I've also enjoyed my time out of football, too," Willard said. "When I got through playing, I felt like I did everything I could do in the game. I would've loved to have won a Super Bowl, though. That's the one thing you can accomplish that would change your life."

Where Have You Gone?

FRANK NUNLEY

On the day he was introduced as new coach of the 49ers, Mike Nolan spoke about some of his memories growing up with his father as the coach.

He then peered into the sizable gathering and saw a handful of his father's former players in attendance. He spotted Frank Nunley, and acknowledged his presence.

"Fudge Hammer!" he said.

In a time when nicknames were still en vogue in the late 1960s and 1970s, Nunley had one of the best of all time. And he owes it all to Stan Hindman, a defensive end who was a first-round pick in 1966, a year before Nunley joined the team.

Nunley, a third-round selection from Michigan, moved into the starting lineup a couple years into his career and solidified the middle linebacker position with his hard hitting.

"I never had the best figure in the world, looking at it from a womanly point of view," Nunley said. "I didn't have the well-defined chest or anything like that."

After witnessing his style of play, Hindman began calling his teammate "Fudge Hammer," because he looked like fudge and hit like a hammer.

"It was fitting," said one longtime fan of the 49ers. "Nunley didn't look hard as nails like Chuck Bednarik, but he indeed made his presence felt to opposing runners."

Nunley was a fixture in the 49ers' starting lineup from 1969 to 1976. His workman-like effort was a great complement to left outside linebacker Dave Wilcox, who would eventually be inducted into the Pro Football Hall of Fame.

Nothing was ever given to Nunley. In fact, it seemed as if the 49ers tried to find someone every season to take his job away from him. But through his gritty determination and solid production on the field, he would not allow it.

"They drafted a middle linebacker in the first three rounds of the draft every year," Nunley said. "I was a third-round pick. So I'd go into training camp, and there would be 15 linebackers there. When I'd make the team, there would be one linebacker backing you up. There was always a sense of urgency to perform, because you were always one play away from never playing again."

Nunley was ultra-tough and did not allow injuries that would keep others out for an entire season to derail him.

On the opening kickoff of the 1967 season, Nunley ran down to make a tackle against the Minnesota Vikings and sustained a torn left knee ligament and shattered cartilage.

FRANK NUNLEY

Linebacker · Michigan · Ht. 6-2; Wt. 230
Born: October 1, 1945 · 49ers career: 1967-1976

Career highlights: Third-round selection in 1967 draft ·
Started at middle linebacker from 1969 to 1976 · Recorded 14
career interceptions, including career-high four in 1974 ·
Invited to play in 1970 Pro Bowl, but was unable to attend due
to knee surgery · Played in 137 games in 10-year career.

His left leg was two inches shorter than his right, Nunley said. However, Nunley did not miss a game as a rookie.

One of his shining moments came later that year when he recorded the first interception of his career, which came against Baltimore legend Johnny Unitas.

In 1970, Nunley played with cartilage problems in his knee. He underwent surgery shortly after the season. Unfortunately, the timing was horrible. Dick Nolan, the coach of the NFC Pro Bowl team that season, asked Nunley to play in the game after one of the team's selected players was sidelined. It was the only time Nunley was asked to play in the Pro Bowl, and he was physically unable.

His final year in the league, 1976, he sustained an identical injury but to his right knee.

"It was the last preseason game against the Rams, and I tried to jump over [center] Rich Saul and I caught the tip of my shoe on his helmet," Nunley said. "It turns out I tore my ACL again, and I had bone chips, too."

There's one thing Nunley learned from experiencing knee injuries at either end of his career.

"Being a step slower in your 10th year in the league is hazardous to your health," he said.

Nunley said his decrease in foot speed caused numerous other injuries throughout his final season. He sustained a broken carotid bone near his ear lobe, as well as a broken nose and various deep contusions that sent him to the hospital after games.

But after breaking the carotid bone, Nunley said it looked as if his season was over. Coach Monte Clark asked him to suit up for the game as a morale boost to his teammates.

"We were playing Minnesota the next week, and the starter goes down, so guess who they send in to play?" Nunley said. "I'd probably be making $2.5 million today like the other linebackers, and they would be trying to protect their investment."

Of course, Nunley never made $2.5 million, but he did earn a handsome living. He said he remembers the late Leo Nomellini, whose Hall of Fame career ended in 1963, asking how much money Nunley was earning.

"I'd say $65,000, and Leo would say, 'Oh, you're killing me,'" Nunley said. "It's the same today. These guys now are making a ton of money. When I played you had to work in the offseason."

However, Nunley isn't complaining too much. The last contract he signed with the 49ers was very generous—with a huge assist from the fledgling World Football League.

Nunley's contract expired after the 1974 season, and a friend of his from Michigan had invested in the Detroit Wheels of the WFL. The Wheels drafted Nunley, and he was sent a "World Football League" gym bag. He made sure he showed up in the team's offices in Redwood City more often than usual that offseason to show off his bag.

"I let Jack White, the [49ers] general manager, know that I'd be flying to Detroit," Nunley said. "He said he wouldn't let me leave until I re-signed. He signed me to a contract where I made $100,000 a year for three years and I had a $30,000 bonus. It was nice to have the upper hand."

*Frank Nunley, a rough-and-tumble player with the
49ers, is now working in the field of 'high tech.'*
Photo courtesy of Dan Audick

After his playing career, Nunley, a physical education major at Michigan, considered entering the coaching field. Instead he went a different route. Nunley works in the electronics industry with his son, Frankie, selling electronic manufacturing for Sanmina-SCI, a Fortune 500 company. He got into that line of work in 1980.

"I had no technical experience whatsoever," said Nunley, who lives in Los Altos Hills with Lynn, his wife since 1968. "Now I can talk pretty legitimately about what's going on. I might not have gotten in on the 'high-tech' ground floor, probably more like the second floor."

Although Nunley said his knees now "look like a road map," he has maintained good health. He walks the 7.8 miles to his office in about 90 minutes once or twice a week and he plays golf on the weekends without the use of a cart.

CEDRICK HARDMAN

Defensive end Cedrick Hardman was such a dominant player, even the president of the United States could not devise a method to outwit him.

President Richard Nixon, a big Washington Redskins fan, called coach George Allen the night before a playoff game in December 1971 against the 49ers.

"I'd like to see you run a flanker reverse with Roy Jefferson against the 49ers," Nixon advised Allen, reported television broadcaster Bill Brundige more than three decades ago.

The Redskins had the momentum in their playoff game against the 49ers, leading 10-3. They had the ball on the 49ers' eight-yard line with less than 30 seconds remaining in the first half. Perhaps taking the president's suggestion, the Redskins unveiled their reverse to Jefferson.

The trickery did not fool Hardman, as he threw Jefferson for a 12-yard loss.

The 49ers then blocked the field goal to maintain a seven-point deficit entering the third quarter. The 49ers' offense got going in the second half, and Hardman sacked Washington quarterback Billy Kilmer on the final play of the game to preserve a 24-20 victory at Candlestick Park.

The next week, Hardman had a hand in five sacks in a 14-3 loss to the Dallas Cowboys in the NFC Championship Game.

"If someone were to get five sacks in the NFC Championship Game today, they'd take his shoes and helmet and send them straight to Canton," Hardman said. "But we lost that game, so it wasn't a big deal."

Hardman had one of the best seasons for any defensive player in 49ers history in 1971, as he recorded a team-record 18 sacks in 14 regular-season games. But that was before the sack was an officially recognized statistic.

Hardman says the NFL does not give the past generations of players as much credit as they deserve, because they want everyone to believe the quality of football is better now than it has ever been.

"One of the things you notice is that they're trying to make you think you're watching the best there ever was," Hardman said. "Television has taken control. The television networks have spent a lot of money for the rights to televise those games, and they try to dress it up like Hollywood. You see guys doing superficial stuff. They're exuberant when they make average plays, and they're highly overpaid to begin with."

CEDRICK HARDMAN
Defensive end · North Texas State · Ht. 6-3; Wt. 250
Born: October 4, 1948 · 49ers career: 1970-1979

Career highlights: First-round selection in 1970 draft · Career and single-season 49ers record holder in sacks. Credited with 112.5 sacks during 10-year 49ers career, including 18 in 1971 · Selected to Pro Bowl in 1971 and 1975 · First-team All-NFL in 1971 · Second-team All-NFL in 1972 and 1975 · Played 171 games in 12-year career · Played final two seasons (1980-1981) with Oakland Raiders.

Hardman is nonplussed the NFL only recognizes the quarterback sack as a statistic since 1982, therefore ignoring his accomplishments, as well as some of the other great pass rushers in the 1970s, 1960s and before.

"How dare they say that the sack began in 1982," he said. "With all the modern technology they have, you're telling me they can't go back and find out how many sacks each player had?"

Hardman worked hard for every sack he achieved in his career, which is one reason he was particularly appalled when he saw the manner in which New York Giants defensive end Michael Strahan broke the Mark Gastineau's "official" NFL sack record in 2001.

"When you see stuff like [Brett] Favre and Strahan looking like they're collaborating on a sack so he can get the record, it makes you sick," Hardman said. "All the work that you put into it and the love you have for it, and then you see them do something like that just so it can be in print."

To the 49ers' credit, their official team records list the sack as going back to 1971, the year after Hardman broke into the league. However, Hardman said the 49ers shorted him 7.5 sacks during his ten seasons with the team. Hardman is still the team's all-time leader with 112.5 sacks—a total he said should be 120.

Hardman said he should know how many sacks he had. While the rest of the league did not start counting sacks until his playing days were over, he began his tally "from the first time I wound up in the pocket."

With a playing weight around 240 pounds, Hardman was a dominant speed rusher who would terrorize left tackles with his quickness off the edge.

"I had a wide variety of moves, but all the moves would revolve around my favorite move," he said. "I'm looking to get off the ball and when I do, all bets are off. I'm going to get to the quarterback."

Hardman looks back fondly at the days of the "Gold Rush," when the 49ers' front four defined the team. In 1976, Hardman, Tommy Hart, Cleveland Elam, and Jimmy Webb led the way for a team-record 61 sacks in 14 games.

"What is interesting is that I saw where the Atlanta Falcons led the league [in 2004] with 48 sacks," Hardman said, "but that was divided among 11 or 12 players [actually, 13]. In 1976, our starting front four had 57 sacks.

"We were the 'Gold Rush.' There are no front fours now. Now you have schemes and zone blitzes, where defensive linemen are dropping into pass coverage. You couldn't have gotten us to do that. We didn't know how to go south, we only went north."

In 12 seasons in the league, including the final two with the Oakland Raiders, Hardman missed only five games. In his first season with the Raiders, Hardman played on a Super Bowl title team.

In 1982, he became the first player signed by the Oakland Invaders of the USFL, doubling as an assistant coach. Hardman has lived in Laguna Beach, in Southern California, since 1983. He did some coaching at Laguna Beach High School, and later joined George Allen's staff at Long Beach State until Allen died in 1990. The school dropped its football program shortly thereafter.

He has remained in good health even after his playing days. In 1985, he began skiing, which he says is the closest thing to the high he felt from rushing the quarterback on a third-and-long. "I was still young, dumb and strong," Hardman said of beginning to ski. "Those are the requirements."

He also worked for a record company and did some work in the theater and movies. In 1972, he had a role in Robert Redford's *The Candidate*. In 1980, he played Big Mean in *Stir Crazy*, starring Richard Pryor and Gene Wilder. He also appeared in *House Party* in 1990.

Hardman stays busy now with a multitude of personal appearances, charity work, and autograph sessions.

DELVIN WILLIAMS

D elvin Williams set team records for the 49ers and Miami Dolphins, and he was the first running back in NFL history to reach one significant milestone. But ask Williams about his proudest accomplishments, and you'll find he eschews mentioning his football heroics.

After arriving at the University of Kansas as an academic non-qualifier, Williams earned a degree in four years in physical education with a minor in biological science. And upon signing with the 49ers in 1974, he was able to move his mother out of the projects of Houston, Texas.

It has not been an easy road for Williams throughout his life, and now he is faced with another big challenge: raising his teenaged grandson alone.

Williams has made a remarkable recovery from being an admitted drug abuser more than two decades ago. At the time, his career was drawing to an end with the Dolphins in 1980, he said he used cocaine to deal with the stresses of life.

"Here in San Francisco, it started out on a social level," Williams said. "The crescendo was in Miami."

In 1981, Williams went into further despair over the fatal heart attack suffered by his mother at age 46. Not wanting drugs to consume him and concerned about his own health and the quality of life, Williams did something about his problem. He sought psychological therapy, which he continued until 1999 when his therapist retired.

Williams has turned his bad experiences into a positive. He ran a non-profit organization for several years, trying to prevent kids from making the same wrong choices he made. He testified before the Senate Committee on Labor and Human Resources in 1989 during hearings to examine treatment and prevention programs. He also served on the board of San Francisco's Haight-Ashbury Free Clinic, and he still makes occasional public appearances.

During his time with the 49ers, Williams established himself as one of the most electrifying runners in club history. He gained 2,966 yards, averaging 4.4 yards a carry, while the club compiled a 24-32 record from 1974 to 1977.

"Those were my best years," Williams said. "I missed it when I went to play for the Miami Dolphins. I just didn't like it down there. It was hot, and you were under close scrutiny, because in those days the Dolphins were the only game in town."

Williams's best statistical game with the 49ers came after the team had gotten out to a surprising 6-1 start in 1976. Williams definitely did his share of the work that day

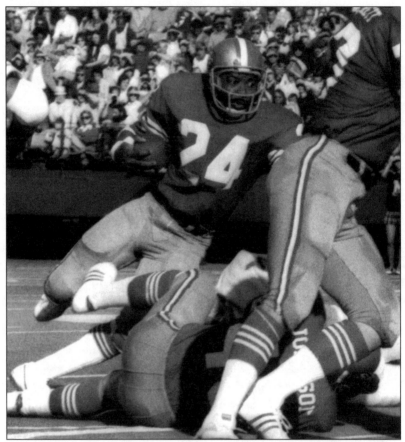

Michael Zagaris photo

DELVIN WILLIAMS
Running back · Kansas · Ht. 6-0; Wt. 197
Born: April 17, 1951 · 49ers career: 1974-1977

Career highlights: Second-round selection in 1974 draft · Led
team in rushing in 1975, 1976 and 1977 · Rushed for a then-
team record 1,203 yards in 1976 with seven touchdowns ·
Rushed for then-team record 194 yards Oct. 31, 1976, vs. St.
Louis Cardinals · Traded to Miami Dolphins in 1978 ·
Rushed for 1,258 yards for Dolphins in 1978, becoming first
player in league history to gain 1,000 yards with two teams ·
Finished career with 5,598 yards rushing on 1,312 rushes and
33 touchdowns · Played 99 games in seven-year career, including final three seasons (1978-1980) with Dolphins.

against the St. Louis Cardinals, but it was not enough. He carried a career-high 34 times for a then-team-record 194 yards and three touchdowns.

However, Williams could not do it alone. Kicker Steve Mike-Mayer missed an extra point and two field goals, including a 23-yarder in the closing minutes of regulation. The 49ers had fumbles on kickoff and punt returns that led to 10 points, including a field goal in overtime of their 23-20 loss.

"I remember that game vividly," Williams said. "I didn't realize I was doing what I was doing, because I wanted to win that game so badly. That was a big game for us."

The next week was equally big, and Williams had another huge performance. This time he rushed for 180 yards against the Washington Redskins, and caught another 99 yards in passes for 279 total yards from scrimmage. But again, the 49ers lost.

The 49ers lost five of their final seven games of the season to finish with an 8-6 record, two games from a playoff spot.

Later that same season, Williams rushed for 153 yards in a 20-16 victory over the Minnesota Vikings on *Monday Night Football.* Also in that game, 49ers fullback Wilbur Jackson gained 156 yards.

Williams's single-game 49ers' rushing record lasted 22 years before Garrison Hearst broke it with a 198-yard performance against Detroit in 1998. Two years later, Charlie Garner gained 201 yards against the Dallas Cowboys.

"Given all of the 49ers success through the years, it's amazing it lasted that long," Williams said. "I'm pleased those records lasted that long."

Williams also set the single-season record of 1,203 yards in 1976, breaking Joe Perry's mark that had stood for 22 years. It was the 49ers' first 1,000-yard rushing performance since J.D. Smith in 1959.

His record lasted until 1984, when Wendell Tyler gained 1,262 yards. The record was subsequently broken by Roger Craig and Hearst.

"I told Wendell that he had to break that record in 14 games," Williams said. "I told him, 'If you break it in 14 games, I'll take you out to dinner. And if it takes you 16 games, you have to take me out to dinner.' It took him 16 games, and I haven't gotten my dinner yet."

But there is one NFL record that nobody will ever be able to take away from Williams. He was the first player in league history to rush for more than 1,000 yards with two different teams, as well as making the Pro Bowl in both conferences. He accomplished the feat after joining the Dolphins.

"I'm proud that I was able to leave a mark on the game," he said.

The 49ers dealt Williams to the Dolphins in 1978 in exchange for Freddie Solomon and a first-round draft pick the 49ers would use on Dan Bunz. Williams paid immediate dividends for Don Shula's Dolphins, as he rushed for a team-record 1,258 yards, breaking Larry Csonka's mark.

That record lasted until Ricky Williams rushed for 1,372 and 1,853 in back-to-back seasons in 2002 and 2003.

Delvin Williams now has a whole new set of challenges in his post-football life.

In the summer of 2004, he gained custody of his 14-year-old grandson, Je'Marcus, who moved from Houston. Although Williams never married, he became a father as a teenager. His daughter, Je'Marcus's mother, has battled substance-abuse issues and is incarcerated, prompting Williams to raise his grandson.

"This is a good thing for him," said Williams, who lives in Mountain View, California. "I see a lot of myself in him. My father wasn't in my life growing up, so I didn't have the guidance of a strong male role model. I can see the benefits of being involved in his life."

Je'Marcus appears to have a bright future as a football player. As a six-foot, 250-pound freshman on the Los Altos High School varsity team in 2004, he was selected first-team all-league as a defensive lineman.

"It's been a change of lifestyle for me," said Williams, who planned to legally adopt his grandson. "I'm easing into retirement, and now I have a 14 year old who I'm responsible for. I've worked with kids over the years in various programs, but I'm fortunate that he's 14 years old and a good kid."

Williams's source of income is from his NFL disability retirement pension. He recently lost a lawsuit that stretched for seven years, in which he sought two years in back pay from the plan. After winning the initial trial ruling, he lost on appeal.

He definitely feels the effects of his seven-year professional career. He has experienced 13 football-related surgeries, including a hip replacement. After his career, he was diagnosed with sleep apnea, and has undergone six surgeries in hopes of fixing the problem.

"I have recurring problems with my neck and back and knees," he said. "Those things catch up with you the older you get. I'm taking care of myself physically. I do yoga and I work out on the treadmill and bike. My physical condition is my No. 1 priority, other than my grandson."

Where Have You Gone?

KEITH FAHNHORST

Keith Fahnhorst remembers what might have been the darkest moment as a member of the 49ers.

He trudged into the locker room at the Pontiac Silverdome after the final game of the 1978 season. The 49ers had just lost to the Detroit Lions, finishing with a 2-14 record.

Head coach Fred O'Connor, who had taken over for the fired Pete McCulley at midseason, stepped in front of the team for some closing words.

"He was saying that we were going to turn it around next year," Fahnhorst said. "He said we were going to go through the toughest training camp ever next year. I remember thinking, 'No, that's not the answer.'"

And indeed, it wasn't.

Owner Eddie DeBartolo, who had bought the 49ers just two years earlier, fired general manager Joe Thomas and O'Connor and hired Bill Walsh to turn things around.

Three years later, Fahnhorst returned to the Silverdome as the starting right tackle in the 49ers' first Super Bowl championship.

"We appreciated it, believe me," Fahnhorst said. "I knew just how rewarding it was, because we knew what it was like to be on the very bottom."

Fahnhorst was one of the club's most respected leaders during his days with the club. He suffered through the bad times of the late 1970s before seeing his patience rewarded with two trips to the Super Bowl.

"He was soft-spoken but a great leader by example," Guy McIntyre said. "He was steady and dependable. He had great flexibility for a man that tall. Guys certainly looked up to him."

"Everybody knew they could count on Keith," Walsh said.

Through most of his career, Fahnhorst was overlooked for league honors. But in 1984, he earned a well-deserved trip to play in the Pro Bowl.

After his 14-year career came to an end after the 1987 season, Fahnhorst has continued to experience life's highs and lows.

In 1976, Fahnhorst was playing left tackle, he got accidentally punched in the side by teammate Delvin Williams, who was trying to slip through a hole during a practice session. Despite feeling extreme discomfort, Fahnhorst continued to practice.

That evening, he started passing blood clots, and went to the hospital to undergo an examination. X-rays revealed Fahnhorst had a ruptured kidney and cysts were discovered.

Michael Zagaris photo

KEITH FAHNHORST

Offensive tackle · Minnesota · Ht. 6-6; Wt. 271
Born: February 6, 1952 · 49ers career: 1974-1987

Career highlights: Second-round selection in 1974 draft ·
Named to NFC Pro Bowl team in 1984 · Starting right tackle
from 1976-1986 · Played on two 49ers Super Bowl-winning
teams (1981 and 1984) · Bobb McKittrick Award winner in
1981 and 1986 · Played 193 games in
14 seasons, all with the 49ers.

He was diagnosed with polysystic kidney disease. Fahnhorst was told that he would eventually need a transplant or dialysis.

"I don't remember that," Williams said recently of the practice-field play. "If he said it happened, it happened. I'm going to have to tell him I'm sorry. But hopefully it was a blessing in disguise."

In 2001 when his health was beginning to fail, he went on the transplant list.

Fahnhorst, who lives in the Minneapolis suburb Eden Prairie, Minnesota, tried to go on about his life as best he could. He still attended his Bible study class, a group of about 15 men who had been meeting regularly for nearly four years.

The tight-knit group did not encourage newcomers, because they thought they had something special and did not want to ruin it. "My wife calls it the 'Coffee Clutch,' because we do more gossiping than anything else," he said.

Apham Nnaji, who had been in the United States about 10 years after immigrating from Nigeria, was invited by one of the other members to attend the group.

"He saw my Super Bowl ring and asked about it," Fahnhorst said. "I told him that I used to play for the 49ers, then I took it off and showed it to him."

But when Nnaji informed Fahnhorst that he was a big fan of the Raiders, Fahnhorst kiddingly snatched the ring away from his new acquaintance. They enjoyed their interaction with each other but did not spend a lot of one-on-one time, Fahnhorst said.

Fahnhorst was unable to make the next Bible study. Nnaji inquired about the football player and was told Fahnhorst was not feeling well because he needed a kidney transplant.

Unbeknownst to anybody else, Nnaji decided to go through the screening process at the University of Minnesota. He didn't think much would come of it because he's a black man and Fahnhorst is white, but he soon learned he was a perfect match as a kidney donor.

Still, Nnaji had to do some soul-searching, because he did not believe in organ donation because of religious reasons. Nnaji's wife disagreed, and the two discussed the situation.

Fahnhorst, who is the senior vice president/investments at Piper Jaffray, was in Indianapolis meeting with some of his clients, when his wife called to ask if his donor had called.

She told him Nnaji had called the house and wanted his number. "He must want something else," Fahnhorst told his wife. At that point, Fahnhorst clicked over to call waiting. It was Nnaji.

"I've decided to give you one of my kidneys," he said.

Fahnhorst could not believe what he had just heard. After the two hung up, Fahnhorst almost immediately called back to thank Nnaji—and ask if he really wanted to go through with it. He then entered the room to meet with his clients.

"It was after an ugly three-year bear market, and I went in there smiling like a big dog," Fahnhorst said. "I told them, 'I hate to be smiling like this, but I just got news that I'm going to be getting a kidney.' It was incredible."

That day, the stock market began to turn, Fahnhorst said.

*Keith Fahnhorst (right) shares a light moment with former
teammate Dan Audick during an alumni gathering in 2004.*
Photo courtesy of Dan Audick

Two days before the surgery was scheduled, Fahnhorst, Nnaji and their wives arranged a meeting.

"We didn't want to make a wrong impression," Fahnhorst said. "We were nervous wrecks. But within the first five minutes, we knew they were the real thing. We wondered, 'Why is he doing this? Is he expecting money?' When we met, we knew they were doing it for all the right reasons. There were no ulterior motives."

Nnaji had been laid off from work shortly before giving up one of his kidneys. He was out of work for six months, and his wife went through a difficult pregnancy. Yet, Nnaji told his new friend, "This has been the best year of my life."

It turned out to be pretty good for Fahnhorst, too. Although he returned to work about three weeks earlier than he admits he should have, Fahnhorst is back to living a normal life.

"I was a little impatient after the operation," Fahnhorst said. "I'm used to having surgery and within four weeks being as good as new. Doctors kept telling me that I'll continue to get better."

EASON RAMSON

Facing 35 years to life in prison, Eason Ramson sat in a courtroom with tears rolling down his face.

Former teammate William "Bubba" Paris pleaded for the judge to give Ramson another chance. He spoke passionately of Ramson's kind and caring side, which Paris had witnessed bubbling to the surface when he gave children presents at Christmas and extended generous handouts to the homeless.

"Bubba talked to the judge for half an hour, and I heard him say things that I had lost touch with," Ramson said. "He talked about the good things I had done in the past. The light started to come on."

He also read the letters former coach Bill Walsh had written on his behalf. Walsh described Ramson as a "fighter" and a "competitor"—qualities he would need to turn his life around.

"He was a good man," Walsh said. "He developed a drug addiction that none of us could help him with."

Said Ramson, "At that point, I felt I had fallen so far, that the road up was too steep for me to climb out."

Ramson was in and out of prison three times. His crack habit had reached $1,000 a day. He was nearly killed twice, and once attempted to take his own life with a drug overdose. He lost two marriages, his oldest son doesn't speak to him, and his youngest son is serving his second prison term.

Yet this is a positive story of one man's quest to turn his life around and affect change in others, too.

Eason Ramson, the former 49ers tight end of five seasons and the last player to wear No. 80 before Jerry Rice, has been clean and sober for six years, as of May 2005. But instead of running from his past, Ramson is more than happy to share all of the uncomfortable details.

"Recovery is an ongoing process," Ramson said. "You don't ever fully recover, but we do regain our respect and regain our lives and move forward. I stay cognizant of where I've been. I don't forget."

Ramson's demons trace back to his childhood in Sacramento, he said, during which he was given up for adoption. He was raised by an abusive father who always told him he would never amount to anything.

EASON RAMSON

Tight end · Washington State · Ht. 6-2; Wt. 235
Born: April 30, 1956 · 49ers career: 1979-1983

Career highlights: Earned roster spot with St. Cardinals in 1978
as undrafted free agent · Signed with 49ers in 1979 · Caught
104 passes in career for 983 yards and five touchdowns ·
Played on 49ers' 1981 Super Bowl champion · Played 85
games in seven-year career, including final
season with Buffalo Bills (1985).

But Ramson did amount to something—earning a roster spot with the St. Louis Cardinals in 1978 after a standout career at Washington State. He admits to caving in to peer pressure after making his first NFL roster.

"I was hanging around people I thought I wanted to be like," Ramson said.

Ramson went to a club with some teammates, including one player he said he had always admired. That player reached into his pocket and produced some cocaine.

"Now you deserve a rich man's high," the player told Ramson.

His experience with cocaine began as experimental, he said. Then it turned to recreational. When he got to the 49ers in 1979, he was regularly using drugs.

"When we'd win games, we'd party," Ramson said. "Remember, in 1981, we won 16 games. I was one of the few who got caught up in it. The more we partied, the more I started to seclude myself and slip away and do it by myself."

In 1983, Ramson clearly had a problem that had come to the attention of the organization. The next season, Walsh traded him to the Buffalo Bills

"When his performance started to fall off, we had to move on," Walsh said. "Unfortunately, that's when he really started to have problems."

After his career concluded with the Bills in 1985, Ramson's life spiraled out of control. He was shot in the back a couple days after robbing a drug dealer. He was nearly killed in another incident involving drug dealers when his head was split open with a golf club. Another time, Ramson said, he overdosed and "wigged out" before police intervened and took him to the hospital.

In 1991, he was convicted of 13 armed robberies at ATMs and sent to prison for 16 months. Following his release he was caught trying to steal a shopping cart full of liquor. He was incarcerated for another 39 months.

He tried to turn his life around in 1996, doing some public speaking and telling people about his past. Unfortunately, he revisited his past.

"I ended up falling off and relapsing, and the embarrassment was huge," Ramson said.

He turned back to drugs. Ramson tried to steal a pair of pants from a department store. When he was caught, he became a candidate for a life sentence under California's three-strikes law.

"My criminality was not sophisticated," he said. "Deep down, it was a cry for help, because I knew I couldn't stop."

And he couldn't turn his life around without reaching out for assistance. Former teammates Paris, Keena Turner, and Eric Wright showed support for him during his darkest hours. And Walsh's encouragement also got him to believe he was capable of turning his life around, Ramson says.

His final sentence in San Quentin's maximum security was 28 months, and he served approximately half of that time before his release. He went into Walden House, an alcohol and drug treatment facility in San Francisco. Ramson took classes on parenting, anger management and conflict resolution, earning certificates in each of those programs.

Now Ramson is making a positive impact on society. He started a non-profit organization called "Pros and Cons For Kids," in which he teams with professional athletes and former convicts to encourage adolescents to make healthy life decisions.

He is also the project administrator at Ella Hill Hutch Community Center in San Francisco, making the commute from his apartment in the East Bay city of Concord daily. He works with the San Francisco School District's truancy program. He is also an administrator in Young Academic Achievers, which serves 180 kids in four after-school programs.

Ramson knows what it is like to be left behind as a child. His biological mother gave him up for adoption. But he reconnected with her and built a close relationship. However, when she remarried, her husband did not allow Ramson to come to the house. After his death, he and his mother reestablished a strong bond, Ramson said.

Ramson said he made the same mistakes with his two sons that his adoptive father made with him. But there is proof Ramson is getting it right. Taylor, his daughter, was born June 1, 1997. He has joint legal custody of his daughter, and he said he is determined to be a good father.

Eason Ramson is now making a positive difference in the community after struggling for control of his own life.
Photo courtesy of Dan Audick

The Northern California Chapter of the NFL Alumni Association has recognized his contributions with "The Eason Ramson Celebrate a Drug-Free Life Award."

He doesn't follow football much anymore, but Ramson will never forget playing in the Super Bowl. He was part of the 49ers team that defeated the Cincinnati Bengals in Super Bowl XVI.

"I remember the Super Bowl—that stands out for me—and all the work we did to get there," Ramson said.

Although his time in the NFL might have contributed to his myriad of problems, Ramson also realizes that the relationships he forged with the 49ers helped save him from himself. He is eternally grateful to Paris, Turner, Wright, and Walsh.

"They helped me connect with the inner drive that I needed to make it to the NFL," Ramson said. "I used that same vigor, work ethic and drive in my recovery. I had my challenges to get there, of course, and now I can use those qualities on a daily basis in my new life."

Where Have You Gone?

DWIGHT CLARK

Dwight Clark admits he was probably never more nervous during a football game than when he ran out as part of the "hands team" to guard against an onside kick late in Super Bowl XVI.

After all, if Clark flubbed the onside kick and the Cincinnati Bengals somehow scored the winning touchdown in the closing seconds, everything would have been different.

"The Catch" would have become a mere footnote in the annals of NFL history. Instead of hailed for one of the most dramatic plays in NFL lore, Clark could have been the goat on the game's biggest stage.

"All I could think about was that unfortunate onside kick against Dallas [in January 1973] when they fumbled it," said Clark, referring to the infamous play involving former 49ers player Preston Riley.

"Running across the field, that's all I could think about. Back then, the kickers didn't know how to slam that ball into the turf and have it pop up in the air 40 feet. Instead, it just bounced along the ground twice and came right to me. I caught it, and Ronnie Lott was my protector. Nobody was going to get to me. Ronnie started screaming, 'We're Super Bowl champs!'

"I just tossed the ball to the ref. I wish I had kept that ball."

The 49ers' first Super Bowl title capped a remarkable two weeks for Clark, whose life would forever be changed.

Two weeks earlier, there was little indication Clark would be physically capable of making the most memorable play in team history. In the days leading up to the NFC Championship Game, Clark had been bed-ridden with the flu.

In fact, on the final drive, Clark was on the brink of exhaustion. During a timeout with 1:15 remaining in the game, Clark fell to one knee, fighting to get his breath. A team trainer stood next to him, and Clark struggled to his feet, he waved off a team doctor.

"I couldn't freakin' breathe," Clark said. "I didn't have any energy because of the flu. I'd been sick for two weeks."

Yet just three plays later, Clark launched his six-foot-four-inch frame as high as possible to come down with Joe Montana's pass. Clark snared the ball with his fingertips, and seemed to lose control for a split-second before securing it in his hands for the touchdown that propelled the 49ers to a 28-27 victory.

Michael Zagaris photo

DWIGHT CLARK

Wide receiver · Clemson · Ht. 6-4; Wt. 215
Born: Jan. 8, 1957 · 49ers career: 1979-1987

Career highlights: Selected in 10th round of 1979 draft · Led team in receiving yards 1981-1983 · Pro Bowl in 1981 and 1982 · First-team All-NFL in 1982 and 1983 · Sports Illustrated Player of the Year in 1982 · Made "The Catch" in closing minute to defeat the Dallas Cowboys in the 1981 NFC Championship Game · Len Eshmont Award winner in 1982 · Ranks fourth on 49ers' all-time list with 506 catches for 6,750 yards and 48 touchdowns · Played 134 games in nine-year career, all with the 49ers · Jersey No. 87 retired in 1988.

"And for all those Dallas fans who think that was a fluke, I have a tape in my possession that proves it wasn't," Clark said.

Clark said NFL Films sent him a clip in which Walsh's instructions to Montana before the final play are clearly audible. The play was called "Sprint Right Option." The play was designed for Montana to roll to his right. The first option on the route was receiver Freddie Solomon, who lined up in the slot and ran an "out" to the end-zone pylon. Then, Walsh tells Montana, "Look for Dwight, and [if he's not open] throw it away."

"Joe put it where I could go get it," Clark said.

As for the historical significance of "The Catch," Clark disputes the notion that the Super Bowl was anticlimactic.

"That was a big game, because it helped us get to the Super Bowl, and the 49ers had never been there before," Clark said. "But it wouldn't have near the impact if we'd lost the Super Bowl. The game against Dallas just wouldn't have had the same meaning."

There is no debating the importance of "The Catch." However, there seems to be some question about the whereabouts of the historical football that Clark snatched out of the air.

About 10 years after "The Catch," former 49ers director of public relations Jerry Walker found the ball, which Clark had handed to him after the game, while cleaning his garage for his daughter Kelly's 11th birthday party. Walker immediately returned the ball to Clark, who then displayed it in his restaurant.

"When I sold the restaurant, it took up residence in a box in my closet," Clark said.

But was it really the ball? In 2005, *Sports Illustrated* reported that longtime 49ers season-ticket holder William F. McDonagh Jr. claimed he bought the ball for $50,000 in 2002 from Jack McGuire, who was a ball boy on the sideline. McGuire retrieved the ball after Clark spiked it in the end zone. McGuire told the magazine, "I gave Dwight a ball, but it wasn't *the* ball." McGuire signed an affidavit at the time of the sale, attesting to the ball's authenticity.

Clark says he is still confident he owns the real ball, saying, "Was the guy dishonest then or dishonest when he signed the affidavit? If he did what he said, I don't know why he would do that to me at that time. But I could see why he would make up a story later on to make some money."

Clark played nine seasons for the 49ers and retired as the 49ers' all-time leader with 506 career receptions. He made the Pro Bowl twice and was named *Sports Illustrated's* Most Valuable Player in the strike-shortened 1982 season. The 49ers retired his number 87 in 1988.

He continued to work with the 49ers as a marketing consultant in 1989 and worked his way to become the team's vice president/general manager from 1995 to '98.

During Clark's watch, the 49ers continued to be Super Bowl contenders every season. The year after he left the organization, the 49ers failed to make the playoffs for the first time in eight years. When Clark and team president Carmen Policy joined the Cleveland Browns, the new 49ers regime regularly criticized them for the way they had managed the salary cap.

Dwight Clark provided 49ers fans with 'The Catch,'
and he also kept the 49ers as a contender every
season during his run as general manager.
Photo courtesy of Dan Audick

"It was Carmen's philosophy, and I agreed with it: Steve [Young] and Jerry [Rice] were special, and as long as they were playing at a high level, we were going to continue to try to win," Clark said.

Even in 2004, before he was fired, 49ers general manager Terry Donahue continued to blame the team's salary cap problems on Policy and Clark, who had left six years earlier.

"As you know in this business, people are going to point fingers to take the blame away from them," Clark said. "All I know is that every year, we were in the running for the Super Bowl. And after two years, they were back in the running again [in 2001]."

During his time in charge of the 49ers, Clark had his personal differences with Walsh. After leaving the Browns in 2001, Clark reports he is back on good terms with the man who took a chance and drafted him in the 10th round of the 1979 draft.

"We're real good with each other," Clark said. "We've kissed and made up."

The light went on for Clark, he said, when he was with the Browns. Policy made an observation.

"You want to run things too much like Bill Walsh," Policy told Clark.

"And I thought, 'I've tried as hard as I can to run things like Bill Walsh,'" Clark said. "Maybe I was too harsh on Bill."

Walsh said he and Clark have a "great" relationship, similar to what they experienced as coach and player.

"He was a terrific guy to work with," Walsh said. "He was really a team leader. He brought a lot of vitality to the team when he was playing. I was probably as close to him as I was with any player.

"Maybe later there was some professional resentment of some kind—whatever it was," Walsh said. "I just wish I could've had a chance to work with Dwight a little, because he didn't get any seasoning at all [before becoming 49ers general manager]."

After leaving the Browns in 2001, Clark and his wife, Ashley, settled in his hometown of Charlotte, North Carolina. In 2004, he became a partner in a construction company that builds houses in South Charlotte. He also remains busy with personal appearances.

Although he has no desire to return to the grinding NFL lifestyle, he has once again found joy on the football field. He coaches a Pop Warner team, on which his son, Mac, plays.

"We ran a mini-West Coast Offense for nine- and 10-year-olds," Clark said, laughing. "People would come watch us play because we're the only team in the league that airs it out." His two older kids, daughter Casey and son Riley, are college students in Massachusetts.

Now that he's out of professional football, he can spend more time with his youngest child, and he can return to being a devoted follower of the 49ers.

"I'm a 49er until the day I die," Clark said. "I don't get a chance to read a lot about them, but I always watch them every chance I get. I still have my 49ers hat that I put on whenever I go anywhere."

JOE MONTANA

Joe Montana, a man who never seemed surprised by anything he saw on the football field, was shocked when he visited his doctor for a routine checkup in 2002.

Perhaps the greatest quarterback of all time, and a player nicknamed "Joe Cool" for his unflappable demeanor during tense times, learned he had abnormally high blood pressure and cholesterol.

Since that time, Montana has engineered a drive to bring awareness to the subject. He experienced no symptoms, and he discovered he might have suffered a heart attack if he had not gone in for a checkup when he did.

"I didn't expect to have it," Montana said in a television interview during Super Bowl in Jacksonville, Florida, in February 2005. "I was going in for my yearly physical, and I found out I had extremely high blood pressure. I felt fine. I didn't have any symptoms. It's called the silent killer."

Montana has stayed mostly out of the limelight since his playing days concluded. He did a one-year stint as a studio analyst in NBC-TV, but that job was taking too much time away from his wife, Jennifer, and their four children.

In 2000, he was named to the Pro Football Hall of Fame, along with teammate Ronnie Lott, former 49ers linebacker Dave Wilcox and Raiders defensive lineman Howie Long.

Montana, the most popular player in the history of the 49ers, symbolized the organization's halcyon days.

He was a no-nonsense performer who would allow himself only an arms-straight-up touchdown signal—and an occasional fist-pump—as a celebration for another scoring pass. And he always saved his best performances for the most pressure-packed situations.

Named as the Super Bowl Most Valuable Player a record three times, Montana's performances while going 4-0 were legendary.

In fact, the only Super Bowl in which he was not named MVP was the one in which he engineered the game-winning drive in the closing minute that culminated with his touchdown pass to John Taylor to beat the Cincinnati Bengals in Super Bowl XXIII.

In his four Super Bowl victories, Montana completed 83 passes to 18 different receivers. He completed 68 percent of his passes for 1,142 yards. Amazingly, he threw 11 touchdowns and no interceptions.

"Joe Montana could put a game plan into work like few humans have ever been able to do—or ever will be able to do," former 49ers tight end Russ Francis said. "He was

Brad Mangin photo

JOE MONTANA

Quarterback · Notre Dame · Ht. 6-2; Wt. 197
Born: July 11, 1956 · 49ers career: 1979-'92

Career highlights: Inducted into Pro Football Hall of Fame in
2000 · NFL Most Valuable Player in 1989 and 1990 · Sports
Illustrated's Sportsman of the Year in 1990 · Super Bowl MVP
three times · Named to NFL's All-Decade team of the 1980s ·
Holds NFL postseason records for completions (460), attempts
(734), yards passing (5,772), touchdowns (45) and 300-yard
passing games (six) · Led 49ers to four Super Bowl titles ·
Len Eshmont Award winner in 1986 and 1989 · Selected to
eight Pro Bowls, including seven with the 49ers · Played 192
games in 15-year NFL career, including final two seasons with
Kansas City Chiefs · Jersey No. 16 retired in 1997.

uncanny in what he was able to do. When you're watching film, you'd see him look at the first receiver. He may not have even been looking at the second and third options, but he's located them. Then he could look at No. 4 and go back to No. 1. Most quarterbacks look at No. 2 and then just get rid of the ball."

Montana won back-to-back NFL Most Valuable Player awards in 1989 and 1990, while leading the 49ers to consecutive Super Bowl titles. He still holds NFL playoff records for most completions (460), yards passing (5,772) and touchdown passes (45).

When asked recently what makes a quarterback great, Montana answered, "Performing under pressure and handling the pressure. You have to handle yourself during a game. Some guys practice like All-Americans, but they can't play."

With the New England Patriots doing in the 2000s what the 49ers did in the 1980s, there are a lot of parallels being drawn between New England quarterback Tom Brady and Montana. Brady led the Patriots a third Super Bowl title in February 2005. He has won two Super Bowl MVP awards, but that's not where the similarities end, Montana said.

"Our paths are somewhat similar, and that's where the comparisons come out," he said. "Both of us were somewhat overlooked in the draft. And the next thing you know, I won Super Bowls, and now he's winning Super Bowls. He also has a certain calmness about him."

Initially there were plenty of doubts whether Montana could play, even though he had a standout career at Notre Dame. Every team in the NFL passed on him at least twice before the 49ers selected Montana with their third-round selection in the 1979 draft.

Montana saw limited time behind Steve DeBerg as a rookie, but he moved into the starting lineup in 1980. In a December 7 game against the New Orleans Saints, Montana gave a crowd of 37,949 at Candlestick Park a hint of what they could come to expect in the decade to follow.

The 49ers overcame a 35-7 halftime deficit, rallying for a 38-35 overtime victory. The 28-point comeback victory still stands as the greatest come-from-behind win in NFL history.

A lot more people were watching just 13 months later when Montana helped the 49ers launch their dynasty with the game-winning drive against the Dallas Cowboys in the NFC Championship Game.

Although Montana threw three interceptions in the game, it was his third touchdown pass of the game that would forever go down in 49ers lore.

The 49ers took over trailing by six points with four minutes, 54 seconds remaining in the game. The team masterfully drove the length of the field to score the winning points on Montana's off-balance throw to the back of the end zone to a leaping Dwight Clark.

"I don't think I've ever done anything that is amazing," Clark said. "Now, what Joe did is amazing, and what Bill [Walsh] did on that last drive is amazing. He was calling runs when everybody expected us to pass."

Montana had already led the 49ers to two Super Bowl titles when Walsh started making contingency plans in case Montana could not play much longer. In 1986, Montana underwent back surgery and was limited to just eight starts.

The next offseason, Walsh traded for Steve Young to serve as Montana's backup until the transition to the new quarterback could take place. However, Montana had no intention of giving up his starting job.

While Young was getting antsy to take over as the full-time starter, a popular theory abounded that Montana was getting near the end. But in 1987 with Young on the sideline, Montana won the first NFL passing title of his career.

In 1988 and 1989, he was the guiding force behind back-to-back Super Bowls.

Young said the situation was uncomfortable because of the competitive nature of both players, but he said the arrangement clearly worked for the 49ers in those pre-salary-cap days. Ultimately, Young admits he gained a great deal by watching Montana for four seasons.

"It worked out for the 49ers," Young said. "And for me, I took it as a positive in the long run to have that experience. I cannot emphasize the impact of watching and learning from Joe. There is no way I can say with a straight face that a huge piece of the puzzle was not witnessing how you play great football."

In 1991, Montana underwent career-threatening surgery to repair a torn tendon in his throwing elbow. His final appearance in a 49ers uniform came in the home finale on a Monday night against the Detroit Lions.

"My emotions were high playing against Detroit at Candlestick, because I knew it was my last game," he said several years later. "And the thing about it, it was almost my audition tape. At that point, I had to prove to other teams I could still play."

Montana completed 15 of 21 passes for 126 yards and two touchdowns in a 24-6 victory over the Lions. Four months later he was traded to the Kansas City Chiefs. He led the Chiefs to the

Joe Montana's surprise appearance on Alumni Day in 2004 was one of the few things 49ers fans had to cheer about during the 2-14 season.
Photo courtesy of Dan Audick

AFC Championship Game in his first season but was knocked out of a 30-13 loss to Buffalo in the third quarter with a concussion.

Montana and his wife, Jennifer, now live on a 500-acre ranch in Sonoma County, in California's wine country. He entered into a partnership with Beringer to produce wine that was expected to be released in 2005, according to the *San Francisco Chronicle*.

He said in one interview that he is trying to avoid a transplant of his left knee, which is rubbing bone to bone. He also underwent neck surgery in February 2005 because of a pinched nerve.

Montana continues to speak out about high blood pressure and cholesterol awareness, urging people to exercise, eat healthy, and communicate with their doctors.

"I have four kids, and I want to stick around, as do others, so I want to get the word out," Montana said.

KEENA TURNER

Keena Turner, proud owner of four Super Bowl rings, keeps the cherished items in a place you would least expect.

"They're in my sock drawer at home," Turner said, laughing. "But don't take that the wrong way. I have great appreciation, respect and love for the game. My appreciation for what we accomplished grows every year, as far as having perspective. It's just that they don't play a part in my day-to-day life."

There is other symbolism, too.

The Super Bowl rings were never something that players on the 49ers spent much time admiring. Those who did probably did not last on the roster for the next season. After all, the 49ers of the 1980s were moving forward at blinding speed.

The 49ers never stood still to admire their accomplishments.

"People don't realize that it was kind of chaotic," Turner said. "We had gotten so good so fast, and the level of expectations were ridiculous. It was hard to enjoy it in that perspective. It was hard to have any kind of true perspective, because we built this inner monster of expectations.

"It was a mental grind, because it was never enough. You were always geared to want more. It was a strange time. It was a great time."

And Turner was there from the beginning.

In 1980 when the 49ers first showed signs of turning the corner, Turner started four games as a rookie after coach Bill Walsh made him a second-round draft pick. He was the full-time starter at right outside linebacker in 1981 when the 49ers won their first Super Bowl.

"Keena was just a great, great player for many years," Walsh said. "He was the best all-around linebacker in the league for a 10-year period. He could do it all. He was a great blitzer, he tackled well and was tremendous in pass coverage. Keena was a key to those championship teams."

And if you think those words are hyperbole, Walsh backed it up when he re-entered the coaching ranks to work at Stanford University in 1992. Turner received the ultimate validation from his playing career when Walsh asked him to join his Stanford staff as linebackers coach.

"When I retired, I wanted to coach but obviously, when Bill asked, I said, 'Yeah,'" Turner said. "That's just what you do when Bill asks you. I really enjoyed it. The most

KEENA TURNER

Linebacker · Purdue · Ht. 6-2; Wt. 211
Born: October 22, 1958 · 49ers career: 1980-1990

**Career highlights: Selected in second-round of 1980 draft ·
Played on four 49ers Super Bowl-winning teams · Named to
NFC Pro Bowl team in 1984 · Len Eshmont Award winner in
1984 · All-NFL second team in 1982, 1984 and 1985 ·
Played 153 games in 11-year NFL career, all with the 49ers.**

rewarding aspect was working with Bill on that level and experience his whole philosophy from the other side.

"My relationship with Coach has grown over the years. I have so much respect for what he was able to accomplish. He was an artist in a lot of ways. He had the ability to push you to the extent that you'd never otherwise consider."

Turner was a starter on all three of Walsh's Super Bowl teams with the 49ers. When asked to pick his favorite, it is difficult for Turner because each has its own identity, he said.

The first one was, well, the first one. Turner was a 23-year-old kid who was battling a nasty bout of chicken pox for the team's last two games. The 1984 team he said was the best team he was on. And in 1988 and 1989, the 49ers worked into the mix some younger players, such as Charles Haley, Tim McKyer, Don Griffin and John Taylor.

"They attached themselves to what we started and brought along their own personalities," Turner said. "And we, as older players, accepted them."

The first one was obviously the most difficult for Turner, who came down with chicken pox on the Thursday before the NFC Championship Game against the Dallas Cowboys. In the two weeks leading up to the Super Bowl, Turner said he had it everywhere.

"I had them in my mouth, in the crack of my butt and in my throat," Turner said. "It was miserable. I couldn't eat, so I lost 10 to 15 pounds between the NFC Championship Game and the Super Bowl. I was sick as a dog."

Turner could barely function during the Super Bowl, but he still managed to record a sack on Cincinnati quarterback Ken Anderson. There is one widely spread misconception he would like to clear up: Turner did not miss any plays during the famed goal-line stand.

Turner admits there was a miscommunication and he came off the field on a fourth-and-one play from the 49ers' five-yard line. Pete Johnson gained two yards to the three for a first down. Then Turner returned to the field for the entire four-play sequence in which the 49ers held the Bengals scoreless, maintaining a 20-7 lead at the end of three quarters.

Three years later when the 49ers returned to the Super Bowl, it was an unforgettable ride for Turner. He also experienced the birth of his daughter, Sheena, in September, he was selected as a team captain, he won the prestigious Len Eshmont Award, and he was chosen to his only Pro Bowl.

Those who followed the 49ers might find it difficult to believe Turner was chosen to play in the Pro Bowl only once in his career, but he understands how difficult it was to be selected with the class of linebackers in the NFC.

"Would I have wanted more accolades or awards? I guess you want that," Turner said. "But I didn't have a problem with the guys who were making it—Ricky Jackson, Hugh Green and Lawrence Taylor—I respected the hell out of those guys."

Just as his playing style highlighted his versatility, Turner has shown equal ability to do a lot of different things after retiring from the NFL.

Keena Turner still works for the 49ers, and is general manager of a car dealership in Tracy, California.
Photo courtesy of Dan Audick

He has worked as a broadcaster on San Jose SaberCats games on the radio and television for more than a decade, and has developed much respect for the Arena Football League. Turner has also worked the 49ers' televised preseason games, as well as the team's pregame show.

Turner worked for DeBartolo Entertainment and spent time as an employee of the 49ers in the role of player relations, a job Guy McIntyre now holds full-time. Turner serves as the 49ers' alumni coordinator, along with Eric Wright, Jesse Sapolu, Steve Bono and McIntyre.

He also took over as general manager of Tracy Toyota in 2004. Turner is a co-owner of the car dealership, along with Ronnie Lott, Charles Haley and Eric Scoggins, who played linebacker for the 49ers in 1982.

His oldest daughter attends the University of Southern California. He also has a younger daughter and a son. He has been married to his wife, Linda, for seven years.

JIM STUCKEY

An hour after the 49ers had defeated the Dallas Cowboys in the 1981 NFC Championship Game, defensive lineman Jim Stuckey was walking to a sink in the team's jubilant locker room. He was carrying a toothbrush in one hand and a football in the other.

"I'll have this ball the rest of my life," Stuckey told the *San Francisco Chronicle*. "No auction—no nothing. No matter how poor I get, I'll carry that one with me just for its significance."

Obviously, the ball held special meaning. Everybody remembers Dwight Clark's leaping fingertip grab in the end zone. But the victory was not assured until Stuckey, a Clemson teammate of Clark, recovered Dallas quarterback Danny White's fumble near midfield with 30 seconds remaining.

Stuckey ran off the field with the ball held aloft. He was never going to fumble the ball that fortuitously found its way into his hands.

So where is that ball now? Unfortunately, Stuckey has no idea.

"I don't have the toothbrush or the ball," Stuckey said.

Said Clark, "It'll show up on eBay one of these days."

Stuckey had his best intentions for his football. A friend made him a beautiful glass case with copper siding to display the ball on the mantel in his condominium in Clemson, South Carolina. But in 1984 when Stuckey sold the place, the ball never made the move with him.

Stuckey's friend who was in charge of moving many of the condominium's contents lost track of the ball. Its whereabouts are unknown to this day.

"Rats. Unbelievable," Stuckey said. "Somebody has a nice glass case with a football in a closet somewhere. They wouldn't even know what the ball is all about. It's not painted or anything. It's just a football that's never been washed or toweled off. All it has are my fingerprints and Danny White's fingerprints."

The historic football has been taken from him, but Stuckey still holds dear the play that guaranteed the 49ers their first trip to a Super Bowl in team history.

The Cowboys, trailing 28-27, moved to the 49ers' 44-yard line on a long pass to Drew Pearson. They needed 15 yards to set up a potential game-winning field goal by Rafael Septien, whose career-long was 53 yards.

Michael Zagaris photo

JIM STUCKEY
Defensive end · Clemson · Ht. 6-4; Wt. 251
Born: June 21, 1958 · 49ers career: 1980-1986

**Career highlights: First-round selection in 1980 draft ·
Recovered fumble in closing seconds to clinch 1981 NFC
Championship Game victory over Dallas Cowboys · Played on
49ers' Super Bowl-winning teams in 1981 and 1984 · Played
93 games in seven-year NFL career · Finished career
with New York Jets in 1986.**

"I just remember Bill McPherson, our defensive line coach, telling me and Lawrence Pillars to run a stunt," Stuckey said. "Lawrence would go first, and I'd come behind him because he could push people more than me."

Pillars lined up at right defensive tackle, and he cut in front of Stuckey, who would loop around the right side of the Cowboys' line. Pillars flattened Cowboys' right guard Kurt Peterson and got to White before he could throw the ball down the field.

"I saw Lawrence hit Danny White's hand," Stuckey said. "It was in slow motion, like you hear people talk about when there's a car accident or something. I saw the ball fall out, and it was bouncing in slow motion on the ground. I saw it and dove on it."

That's when things quickly got back to regular speed, and Stuckey then processed in his mind what had happened.

"Oh, my God," he said. "We just won the game. We're going to the Super Bowl."

Stuckey played on the 49ers' first two Super Bowl champions but admits those games could not compare to the raw emotion he felt in the NFC title victory over the Cowboys. "That was the most exciting game I was ever associated with," Stuckey said.

A week later in the Super Bowl victory over Cincinnati, Stuckey recorded a sack on the Bengals' first possession of the game.

Stuckey, a first-round pick of the 49ers in 1980, left Clemson as the school's all-time sack leader with 18. The mark lasted three years until William "The Refrigerator" Perry broke it. Stuckey was inducted into the Clemson and State of South Carolina hall of fames in 1995.

Although Stuckey led the 49ers with 8.5 sacks his rookie season, he developed more into a run-stuffer when the team brought aboard such pass-rushers as Fred Dean, Dwaine Board and, later, Charles Haley.

"I have some great memories of the people there and watching the team develop," Stuckey said. "It's something I appreciate a little more as I get older. We didn't have much turnover on that team for a period of time in the 1980s. The nucleus of the team remained intact for a long time, so we developed a lot of camaraderie."

Stuckey played just one game for the 49ers in 1986 before landing on the New York Jets' roster. The following summer he tried to hook on with the San Diego Chargers but was released, bringing his career to an end after seven seasons and 93 regular-season games.

He moved to Charleston, a historic South Carolina seaport village where his grandmother was born and raised. After two years of work in the promotions department for Anheiser-Busch, Stuckey found his way into real estate.

Stuckey is a sales executive for Kiawah Resort Associates, which even in its lean years will do $280 million in sales, he said. He sells property on exclusive Kiawah Island, which has 10 miles of private ocean front and seven golf courses.

In 1991, Stuckey married Beth, one of his best friends from college. Stuckey met Beth in 1978, but they never dated until he moved back to South Carolina after his playing days were over. They have two children.

DAN AUDICK

Dan Audick figured there was a realistic chance he would be on a Super Bowl champion when he reported to training camp in 1981.

But that was only because he was a member of the San Diego Chargers until the 49ers traded for his services in the preseason. The 49ers were in desperate need of a starter at left tackle after Ken Bungarda went down with severe ligament damage to a knee. They tabbed Audick to take over at the most critical spot on the offensive line.

In those days, a trade to the 49ers from the Chargers was seen as something of a football death sentence.

After all, the Chargers were being touted as Super Bowl contenders because of their explosive offense. "Air Coryell," named after head coach Don Coryell, featured three future Hall of Famers in their prime: quarterback Dan Fouts, wide receiver Charlie Joiner, and tight end Kellen Winslow. All-Pro wide receiver John Jefferson rounded out football's most exciting team.

The 49ers, meanwhile, had won just 10 games over the previous three seasons.

"Although my Charger teammates tried to encourage me by telling me about Bill Walsh's great offensive talents, I had not followed Joe Montana's career and knew very little of his potential," Audick said.

Although placed in an unbelievably difficult situation, Audick made the most of the opportunity with the 49ers. At six-foot-three, 253 pounds, Audick was a natural guard. He was one of the 49ers' quickest offensive linemen, a trait the late Bobb McKittrick coveted in his charges. McKittrick, who coached Audick with the Chargers in 1978, also liked his "nice nasty streak."

After acquiring Audick for a third-round draft pick, the 49ers inserted him into the lineup at left tackle, where he protected Montana's blind side. Audick was considered a short-term answer at left tackle, as the 49ers were expected to be at least one year away from being legitimate contenders.

Audick started all 16 games and three postseason games at left tackle in 1981, earning just $42,000. When the 49ers ran out the clock in their NFC Championship Game victory over the Dallas Cowboys, Audick and Montana ran side-by-side off the field as the fans began swarming Candlestick Park in celebration.

In an up-and-down career, his starting role in the Super Bowl XVI victory over the Cincinnati Bengals was the zenith. Audick had been drafted by the Pittsburgh Steelers, traded to the Cleveland Browns and released, then signed by the St. Louis Cardinals, all in 1977.

DAN AUDICK
Offensive lineman · Hawaii · Ht. 6-3; Wt. 253
Born: Nov. 15, 1954 · 49ers career: 1981-1982

Career highlights: Selected in fourth round of 1977 draft by
Pittsburgh Steelers · Traded from San Diego Chargers to 49ers
in 1981 for third-round draft pick · Started at left tackle for
49ers' 1981 Super Bowl-winning team · Played 76 games in
eight-year career · Also played for St. Louis Cardinals (1977,
1983-1984), San Diego (1978-1980).

The Cardinals released him in 1978 before he signed with the Chargers, starting 13 games for the club in 1979 and 1980. But all that was a distant memory in that victorious 49ers Super Bowl locker room in Pontiac, Michigan.

"It was the culmination of a lot of highs," Audick said. "The day I got drafted was a special high. Then you get cut and traded, so there are a lot of ups and downs."

Former teammate Dwight Clark, who would become general manager of the 49ers and Cleveland Browns, reflected back with amazement at what Audick did that season.

"He was not a tackle, but he did his best, so hats off to him," Clark said. "Joe [Montana] and I were just talking about that. Dan was stuck in a difficult position, and we won a world championship with him at left tackle."

Likewise, Audick said he "recalls with awe" what the 49ers' unheralded supporting cast helped the 49ers accomplish. He cited such players as Ricky Patton, Bill Ring, Freddie Solomon, Walt Easley, Amos Lawrence, Johnny Davis, Paul Hofer, Earl Cooper, Charle Young, Eason Ramson, and Mike Wilson as heroes in their own right.

"What that collective group did for the performance of Joe Montana was tantamount to what Tenzing Norgay did for Sir Edmund Hillary," Audick said. "We came together as a very special team."

Indeed, the 49ers had conquered their Mount Everest.

However, Audick did not earn the kind of job security he had hoped to achieve with the 49ers. In 1982, the 49ers were in position to go after a prototype left tackle. With its first pick in the second round, they drafted the six-foot-six and 300-plus pound Bubba Paris from the University of Michigan.

Audick acknowledged he had difficulty with the abrupt manner in which he had been replaced at the left tackle position. He lost his starting job in the strike-shortened 1982 season and was traded back to St. Louis, where he retired in 1984.

"He was a 250-pound starter at left tackle on a Super Bowl team," 49ers coach Bill Walsh said. "But in his mind, he was 310 pounds. He was a great competitor and a stalwart on our team. But when we drafted Bubba Paris, Dan had some real problems with that."

Audick said he later learned from a 49ers scout that the club had targeted Paris as a potential draft pick during the 1981 season. With more than 20 years of perspective, Audick now says, "I had never experienced playing with an offensive lineman of Bubba's size, strength, and athletic ability."

Audick certainly had the athletic ability, but the major knock on him from an early age was his lack of size.

He was the son of a career military officer and had traveled around the world. As his family grew to nine siblings, Audick moved from his birth state of California to France, the New England area, Virginia, Tennessee and Tokyo, Japan, where he got his start playing organized football on the junior varsity of an American high school on a military base.

When his father transferred to Colorado Springs, Audick developed into an all-Colorado offensive lineman for Wasson High School's only state championship team in 1971. Coming from a large family meant that getting a college education would require some sort of financial aid, but few colleges were interested. Despite weighing just 195 pounds, the University of Hawaii offered him an athletic scholarship.

By 1977, Audick had managed to avoid the temptations of Oahu's exotic beaches, survived the long distance from his family, earned his bachelor of business administration, and grew big and strong enough to be drafted in the fourth round.

Retirement certainly has not slowed down Audick, who lives in San Diego. He has found other areas in which to excel while coping with the challenges of a bi-polar medical condition. Audick does not speak about this condition for personal reasons.

A self-described "total recluse," Audick focused on his studies at San Diego State after his NFL career ended. He graduated with his MBA in 1986. He earned a second master's in organizational management at the University of Phoenix in 1996. And in 2004, he became Dr. Dan Audick after earning his doctorate of education in the field of human performance technology from the University of Southern California.

His dissertation focuses on the design and development of offensive play systems that might be more player friendly and increase

Dan Audick has overcome a lot of adversity to be recognized now as 'Dr. Dan.'
Photo courtesy of Dan Audick

learning and performance efficiency and effectiveness. Audick—or "Dr. Dan," as he likes to be called—sent copies to more than 25 people connected to the NFL.

Walsh gave him a call to talk about it. Former 49ers executive John McVay, Patriots coach Bill Belichick, Redskins coach Joe Gibbs, University of Nebraska's coach Bill Callahan, ESPN analyst and former coach Bill Curry and former Miami Dolphins coach Dave Wannstedt, now coach at University of Pittsburgh, wrote notes of thanks for the mailing. In his note, Coach Callahan commented, "It is difficult to put together this type of research, which could be very helpful to our program."

Audick sees a time in the near future when players will be asked to "bring your computer" to the coach's office upon being released.

"By the year 2015, if not much sooner, all NFL teams will replace their traditional three-ring binder notebooks with laptop computers," Audick said. "When that happens, these laptop computers will be capable of generating tens of millions of offensive formations and pass routes. Of course, the learning problem is that nobody will be able to learn all of the patterns and formations. My dissertation uses a geometric procedure to solve this problem. This procedure makes it possible to describe all the formations that you could possibly do."

FRED DEAN

It should come as no surprise that the game that stands out during the 1981 season for Fred Dean was against the Dallas Cowboys.

No, not *that* game against the Cowboys.

When the 49ers faced Dallas on October 11, they had just started to look like a pretty good team. The 49ers won two straight games to improve to a 3-2 record with the Dallas Cowboys looming ahead on the schedule. That is when coach Bill Walsh pulled the trigger on a trade that would transform the 49ers from a pretty good team to the best team in the league.

In the sixth week of the regular season, Walsh sent two draft picks to the San Diego Chargers to acquire Dean, an immensely talented player who was having problems with the team's management.

"We didn't know it at the time, but he turned it around," Walsh said. "It all started in that first game. He did things that shocked everybody."

Coincidentally, the first game in which Dean put on a 49ers uniform was against the Cowboys in front of a rare sellout crowd at Candlestick Park.

"To me, that game was my Super Bowl," Dean said upon reflection in 2001. "Coach Walsh said he was going to ease me into the game. As it turned out, I played almost the whole game and I had a very good day."

Dean recorded three sacks of Cowboys quarterback Danny White, forced two hurried passes and batted down two passes at the line of scrimmage in the 49ers' 45-14 victory after practicing just three days with his new team. The 49ers have sold out every home game since.

Despite playing in just 11 games for the 49ers that season, Dean was chosen as the UPI's NFL Defensive Player of the Year. "Dean-fense" signs and chants became common at Candlestick Park.

"Fred was the best pure pass rusher I've ever seen to this day," 49ers teammate Jim Stuckey said. "He had great technique and quickness. His speed was unparalleled in the league at that time."

Dwight Clark said Philadelphia defensive end Jevon Kearse reminds him of Dean, who was listed at six-foot-three, 227 pounds.

"He was the original 'Freak,'" Clark said. "He's the 1980s version of 'The Freak.' He had those long arms, was fast, undersized and relentless. The elephant position was invented for him."

FRED DEAN

Defensive end · Louisiana Tech · Ht. 6-3; Wt. 227
Born: February 24, 1952 · 49ers career: 1981-1985

Career highlights: Selected in second-round of 1975 draft by
San Diego Chargers · Traded to 49ers in 1981 · Three-time
Pro Bowl selection, including two times with 49ers · Named
NFL Defensive Lineman of the Year in 1981 · First-team All-
NFL in 1981 and 1983 · Recorded 40 sacks in five seasons
with 49ers · Six sacks in 1983 game against New Orleans
Saints · Played in 141 games in 11-year career.

Dean was a naturally gifted player. He smoked cigarettes and rarely stepped inside the team's weight room. He was not physically imposing by NFL standards, yet opponents and teammates alike marveled at his strength.

"Fred would bench press 300 pounds 20 times, and this is a guy who never lifted weights," Stuckey said. "Then he'd say, 'That's it for the month.' And he was as fast as any wide receiver we had."

Dean capped that electric first season with a sack of Cincinnati quarterback Ken Anderson in the 49ers' 26-21 victory in Super Bowl XVI.

In five seasons with the 49ers, Dean recorded 40 sacks, ranking seventh on the team's all-time list. He racked up 93.5 sacks for his career, clearly establishing himself as a dominant player in his era. Although he's received some support from influential members of the football media, Dean has never made it to the final ballot in the Pro Football Hall of Fame selection process.

Dean's best season came in 1983 when he recorded 17.5 sacks, including a then-NFL record six sacks in a 27-0 victory over the New Orleans Saints. The next season he missed the 49ers' first 11 games in a contract dispute before Willie Brown, who would eventually become San Francisco's mayor, offered to mediate the talks to resolve the stalemate.

Teammate Keena Turner once described Dean in baseball terms, saying he was like a team's top relief pitcher in a close game.

"If we were trying to protect a lead or we were close behind, Deano in the fourth quarter was a machine," Turner said.

While Dean was playing he had to cope with frequent migraine headaches. He said his problems started in 1976 when he ran head first into a camera cart on the sideline of a game. Since his retirement, the headaches have gotten increasingly prevalent, perhaps exacerbated by the other problems in his life.

Dean lost his automotive repair shop in San Diego after an IRS audit in the early 1990s. He also experienced acute back problems, along with his migraines, forcing him to pay numerous costly visits to hospital emergency rooms.

He has been diagnosed with migraines, cluster headaches and post-traumatic headaches, most likely from numerous concussions he sustained throughout his career. With his medical costs escalating and unable to work because of his physical condition, Dean was forced to sell his two Super Bowl rings at a San Diego pawn shop.

"That was a difficult thing to do," Dean said. "It still hurts. But under the circumstances, you got to do what you got to do. It really bothered me a lot. I was planning on one day trying to retrieve them. I went back to get them at the pawn shop, and the guy had let them go. I don't know where they are now. I didn't want to sell them in the first place, but with the bills piling up, I had no choice."

Dean and his family moved back to his home state of Louisiana, where he finds the heat and humidity more agreeable with his physical problems. He has attended seminary school in the area.

"I got into the school and started to hear the Word," Dean said. "A little light came on, and it all started to make sense."

BILL RING

It did not look good when free-agent running back Bill Ring collided with 49ers teammate Freddie Solomon during a warmup drill at training camp in 1981.

Solomon was knocked unconscious by the force of the impact, and Ring was obviously dazed as he laid sprawled out in front of a sizable crowd of onlookers at Sierra College in Rocklin, California.

"I'm on the ground, about ready to get up, and someone says, 'Wait a minute, something's wrong with his hand,'" Ring recalls.

Ring's middle finger was "split open like a ripe plum," he said. Because of the injury, the 49ers had to place him on injured reserve, which back then was not a season-long sentence.

If it sounds as if the injury was bad luck for Ring, you would be mistaken.

"That injury might have saved my career," he said. "That made them keep me with the team longer. They might have cut me if it weren't for that injury."

After all, Ring was not the kind of player to turn heads with his physical stature or overwhelming talent. He was the kind of player who needed time to demonstrate all his intangibles. The more you watched Ring play, the more you appreciated him.

Those traits have carried over into his post-football life. A successful businessman since getting into the field full-time in 1987, Ring now works in San Francisco as senior vice president at Capital Guardian Trust Company.

Ring, a five-foot-10, 215-pound dynamo, always dreamed as a youngster growing up in South Bend, Indiana, of playing for an NCAA Division I college as a steppingstone into the NFL.

He relocated to the Bay Area at age 10 when his father, in the insurance business, took a job in San Francisco. Although he had offers to play at Division II schools out of high school, he enrolled at College of San Mateo instead. He played there two seasons before going to Brigham Young University.

"I was a catholic," Ring said, "but you know what they say: When in Rome, do as the Romans do; and when in Provo, do as the Mormons do."

Ring was not drafted after his senior season, but the Oakland Raiders signed him as a free agent in 1979. He participated in a three-day minicamp and was released, bringing his Raiders career to an end before he even put on pads.

Michael Zagaris photo

BILL RING

Running back · Brigham Young · Ht. 5-10; Wt. 205
Born: December 13, 1956 · 49ers career: 1981-1986

Career highlights: Earned roster spot in 1981 as free agent ·
Standout special-teams player · Gained 732 yards and seven
touchdowns on 183 career rushing attempts · Named winner
of Len Eshmont Award in 1983 · Member of two Super Bowl-
winning teams with 49ers · Played 69 games
in six-year career with 49ers.

"I would've loved to have been a Raider," Ring said. "Things were a little different over there. I'll never forget seeing Jack Tatum in the shower smoking a cigarette. I'll never forget that for as long as I live."

After getting released, Ring returned to BYU to finish his degree and work as a graduate assistant coach under head coach Lavell Edwards. Ring majored in finance and required a minor, in this case geology, to receive his diploma.

Niners public relations assistant Brian Billick, who was a graduate assistant at BYU and would later become head coach of the Super Bowl-champion Baltimore Ravens, told Ring about a 49ers tryout in Redwood City in 1980. About 400 players showed up, and Ring was one of three or four to get an extra workout. However, the 49ers did not sign him.

He hooked on with the Pittsburgh Steelers and made it to the next-to-last cut. During his time with the Steelers, Ring became friends with overachieving running back Rocky Bleier. The Winnipeg Blue Bombers of the Canadian Football League gave Ring a two-week tryout.

Through it all, Bleier told Ring he was good enough to play in the NFL. So when the Blue Bombers offered Ring a four-year contract, he said, "No, thank you."

Over the course of the next year, Ring got even more serious about sticking in the NFL. He worked out four or five hours a day and got his weight up to 215 or 220 pounds. Finally, the 49ers agreed to bring him to training camp in 1981.

That was when his fortunate injury happened.

Ring was activated for the third game of the regular season, and he came through with a good game on special teams. Afterward coach Bill Walsh released Ring, but assured him he would make some roster adjustments and he would be back on the team in 24 hours.

Finally a week later, he got the anticipated call. Ring stuck on the roster for the next six seasons. But nothing can top that first season, which ended with a Super Bowl title.

"I had to pinch myself," Ring said. "It demonstrates that if you have passion about something, you have to keep with it and believe in yourself, because not a lot of people will do it for you."

Ring was a fan favorite because of his scrappy style. He was also a favorite inside the locker room, being named the winner of the prestigious Len Eshmont Award in 1983.

"Bill was a solid, dependable football player who had tremendous courage," Walsh said. "He thought clearly throughout the game. He was a strong, tough runner and a tremendous special teams player. In tough situations, I knew we could totally count on him."

Since nothing came easy for him during his career, it was only appropriate even the process of his retirement was eventful.

After the 1986 season, a year in which Ring carried the ball just three times but was still a special-teams contributor, Walsh told him to think about retirement. "But before you do that, come visit me in the spring, and we'll talk about it some more," Walsh told him.

When Ring talked to Walsh again before the start of camp, the coach had changed his tune.

"Bill, I don't want you to retire," Walsh told him. "I want you to come to camp and try to make the roster."

Ring said he increased his workouts to be in the best shape of his career. He also hustled like never before during training camp. But it wasn't enough. Walsh again wanted Ring to retire.

"I said, 'I spent nine weeks killing myself, if I can catch on with another team, just release me,'" Ring said. "They released me and I had some inquiries from other teams, but the league went on strike, and I decided to just get on with my life."

During his professional football career, he received training from Dean Witter Financial Services in the offseason and began working at a branch in San Mateo. He became national sales manager at Wells Fargo, and moved on to Robertson Stevens Investments as head of sales and marketing.

In 1999, he went to Capital Guardian Trust, where he is a personal investment counselor, working as a liaison between his clients and the portfolio manager.

"There are certainly things you learn from guys like Bill Walsh that are transferable to the business world," said Ring, who has completed the New York City Marathon three times since getting out of football. "You have to have commitment and dedication in what you do ... the hard work and commitment to excellence sets a standard. That's what I try to do day by day."

MILT McCOLL

Milt McColl did not have to look far to find the model for his professional careers. His father, Bill, went to Stanford University, where he was a two-time All-America football player. While playing end for the Chicago Bears, Bill McColl never lost sight of developing a career outside of football.

Bill McColl has worked as an orthopedic surgeon in Los Angeles, where he is now semi-retired.

Milt McColl was a two-time Academic All-American at Stanford, where both his parents and five siblings went to school. His wife, Cynthia, whom he has been married to since 1983 went to Stanford, and the oldest of his four children was scheduled to begin classes there in the fall of 2005.

During his seven-year career with the 49ers, McColl took classes at Stanford medical school with the intent of becoming an orthopedic surgeon just like his father. However, that is where things differ.

"Our paths were very similar," Milt McColl said. "Only he ended up practicing medicine, and I ended up taking more of the business route."

McColl is president of Boston Scientific Neurovascular, a medical device company with a primary focus on embolic protection for coronary, carotid, and peripheral disease. He has held that position since August 2004. He lives in Los Altos Hills, California.

McColl decided to forego his residency and remain in private industry after taking his first job in that field in 1989, the year after his football career came to an end. He has worked in nine different jobs in such roles as president, CEO, managing director, and general manager.

He had to take his career after football seriously from an early age, because he never seemed convinced he would have any kind of career in the NFL. He went undrafted after his senior season at Stanford but received an invitation to sign with the 49ers as a free agent in 1981.

"I had talked to my dad, and I told him I wasn't sure I'd be able to play in the NFL," McColl said. "He told me that if the opportunity arises, I might want to set myself up for medical school by taking some classes my senior year to get a head start. I'd walk into medical school ahead of the game."

McColl was accepted into UCLA medical school in the fall of 1981, and he was on the waiting list at Stanford. The administration at UCLA did not believe professional football and medical school was a good combination, McColl said. But the same week McColl found out he had made the 49ers, he also received notice from Stanford that he was accepted.

MILT McCOLL

Linebacker · Stanford · Ht. 6-6; Wt. 230
Born: August 28, 1959 · 49ers career: 1981-1987

Career highlights: Earned roster spot as undrafted free agent in 1981 · Member of two Super Bowl-winning teams with 49ers · Fumble recovery in closing minute of first half of Super Bowl XVI led to a field goal · Played 112 games in eight-year NFL career, including final season with Los Angeles Raiders (1988).

"I just wanted to get my signing bonus of $1,000 from the 49ers and get a new stereo," McColl said. "I figured I'd be there for six weeks and that they'd use me as cannon fodder. But a couple guys got hurt."

And the 49ers suddenly had a spot for the six foot six, 230-pounder.

His first couple seasons in the NFL, McColl took night classes. He would typically leave the team's practice facility around 5 p.m., and end up studying for the remainder of the night.

"It was not a lot different than college," he said. "While some of my teammates might have been drinking and carousing at night, I was at home studying and keeping up with my medical work."

In his third season, McColl decided to divide his schoolwork and football into six-month segments.

"He had such a great reputation on the team," then-49ers head coach Bill Walsh said. "He was a big, tall angular guy who played a lot like Ted Hendricks [former Oakland Raiders star]. He was a standout special-teams player, and as time passed became a starter."

While playing football at Stanford, McColl said he continued to be more of a fan of the Los Angeles Rams. After all, the 49ers were not exactly captivating during that time in the late 1970s.

But in 1981, McColl's rookie season, things obviously changed. And McColl made an impact in the 49ers' first Super Bowl victory.

Late in the first half with the 49ers already leading 17-0, Ray Wersching's kickoff was mishandled by Cincinnati returnman Archie Griffin. McColl recovered the loose ball at the four-yard line, setting up Wersching's field goal with two seconds remaining.

"Rick Gervais hit the returner and knocked the ball loose, and there it was sitting at my feet," McColl said. "All I had to do was fall on it."

Then, on the famed goal-line stand, McColl was on the field for the first two plays. On third down, the 49ers changed their defense, and McColl came off the field. That segment of plays turned out to be critical to the 49ers' 26-21 victory, earning them the organization's first Super Bowl title.

"I was only 21 years old," McColl said. "I was just a young kid. I was a free agent who didn't expect to make the team. They had won just 10 games over the previous three seasons, so imagine being on a winning team and then winning a Super Bowl.

"What I remember is the party in the hotel ballroom after the game. Eddie DeBartolo took care of us. He allowed every player to bring four members of his family, so we were able to fully experience it."

McColl also played on the 49ers' Super Bowl team of the 1984 season. But he almost did not make it that far with the 49ers. He found out years after the fact that a trade to the Raiders had fallen through at the last minute.

So in 1988, with his time clearly coming to an end with the 49ers, he signed with the Raiders. After his one season in Los Angeles, McColl retired from the rigors of the NFL to follow in his father's footsteps.

RUSS
FRANCIS

There is not much use for a surfboard in Omaha, Nebraska. He no longer owns a plane or a motorcycle, and his skydiving adventures have been put on hold for a while.

Russ Francis's priorities have changed dramatically since his boy, Riley, was born in 1995. Ah, but don't worry about the good-looking free spirit who resurrected his career in 1982 with the 49ers and played six highly entertaining seasons with the club.

"Peter Pan is alive and well," Francis said. "I have not sold the cottage in Never Never Land."

Francis promises once Riley is on his own, things will get back to normal—or, shall we say, back to abnormal.

"The parachute comes back, as does the motorcycle and a lot of other things," Francis said. "I'm not done with those things by a long stretch."

Today Francis speaks with reverence about former 49ers coach Bill Walsh, who lured Francis out of retirement and orchestrated a trade from the New England Patriots for first- and fourth-round draft choices. But during his playing days, Francis and Walsh did not always see eye to eye on the issues.

Francis grew up in Hawaii, and his parents afforded him many freedoms. As a senior in high school, he was sent to work at the family's ranch in Pleasant Hill, Oregon. He learned to value his independence.

But it seemed Francis was discouraged from doing whatever he pleased when he joined the 49ers.

"I have a tremendous amount of respect for Bill Walsh—it's love and respect," Francis said. "But we had our different ways of looking at things.

"In my mind, life is simple. Bill hired me to play football on Sundays, and that is what I did to the best of my ability. I didn't think surfing big waves, flying airplanes, jumping out of airplanes and riding motorcycles had anything to do with it. He did, and that's where we had a conflict."

The most public battle came in July 1984 when Francis planned to set a speed world record at an air show in Oroville, California. Francis had hoped to shatter the record of 261 miles per hour in the custom-built six-liter plane. Walsh obviously was concerned for his tight end's safety.

"I told him, 'Bill, at 300 miles an hour, there aren't going to be any injuries,'" Francis said.

Michael Zagaris photo

RUSS FRANCIS

Tight end · Oregon · Ht. 6-6; Wt. 242
Born: April 3, 1953 · 49ers career: 1982-1987

Career highlights: Selected in first round of 1975 draft by New England Patriots · Earned three trips to the AFC Pro Bowl before 1982 trade to 49ers · Was starting tight end on 49ers' winning 1984 Super Bowl team · Finished career with 393 receptions for 5,262 yards and 40 touchdowns · Played 167 games in 13-year NFL career · Played eight seasons with New England (1975-1980 and 1987-1988).

Eventually, Francis decided to forego his attempt at the speed record out of deference to Walsh. But he said it wasn't until after his playing days were over that he and Walsh resolved all of their differences.

"You can't cater to each and every free spirit and independent guy," Francis said. "I didn't think it should reach out to the rest of my life. I figured it out later on. I'm very grateful to him."

Walsh says Francis was "just terrific to work with," even though there were certainly times when he drove him crazy.

"I was in for the ride of my life with him," Walsh said. "The motorcycle, the skydiving, there was no way for me to deal with that. I talked to him about it, but he was his own man. All I could do was tease him. He had such a great sense of humor. He could be the butt of the joke, but he was so confident that he couldn't care less."

Francis was a nationally known celebrity when he walked away from the game after the 1980 season because of his disgust with how he said New England executive Chuck Sullivan treated paralyzed receiver Darryl Stingley.

He went to work for ABC-TV, and interviewed Walsh at the Pro Bowl in Hawaii. It was at that time Walsh told Francis, "You only have one time in your life to be able to play the game at this level."

Francis, 28 at the time, had never quite looked at it in those terms. Francis had always done pretty much what he wanted to do when he wanted to do it.

He was a tremendous athlete who never considered his window for greatness would be closing. He set the national high-school javelin record in 1971 with a throw of 259-9, a mark that would stand for 17 years until Art Skipper of Sandy, Oregon, edged him by an inch. The Kansas City Royals drafted Francis in 1974 after seeing him pitch in a summer league while attending the University of Oregon.

Francis played only one season of college football, and that was his junior year. But it was in football where Francis would make his biggest impact.

Patriots coach Chuck Fairbanks took a major gamble and selected Francis in the first round, with the No. 16 overall pick, in the 1975 NFL draft. Ray Perkins, the receivers coach, and Red Miller, the offensive line coach, were responsible for developing the inexperienced young player.

"They'd tell me, 'The bad news is you don't have any good habits, and the good news is you don't have any bad habits,'" Francis said. "They molded me into the image of the tight end they thought they needed."

Francis developed an immediate rapport with Patriots quarterback Steve Grogan, as he was second on the team with 35 catches and four touchdowns as a rookie. The next season, Francis's numbers hit a plateau, but the Patriots had become one of the best teams in the league with an 11-3 record. A disheartening and controversial 24-21 loss to the Oakland Raiders in the playoffs was the most success Francis would experience in the NFL until he joined the 49ers.

In January 1985, Francis caught five passes for 60 yards in the 49ers' victory over the Miami Dolphins in Super Bowl XIX. Francis ranks it as one of his greatest moments but far behind the birth of his son.

Riley's birth forced Francis to take a hard look at the way he lived his life. He does not own a plane or motorcycle, he said, because "I live on a pretty small budget." Now he runs a referral-only consulting operation.

"I lost track of what was really important," said Francis, who experienced some financial problems in the mid-1990s. "I just dealt with whatever happened on that day. Things came into focus when my son was born. When I woke up, I said to myself, 'I should put something away for my son.' That falls into the category of achieving some goals."

Russ Francis looks back on his 49ers days with awe at what the team accomplished.
Photo courtesy of Dan Audick

Francis had another goal in 2000, as he ran for a Hawaii congressional seat. Running as a Republican in the "blue state" against incumbent U.S. Representative Patsy Mink, Francis garnered 36 percent of the vote in the defeat.

He moved to Nebraska, so his wife, Michele, could be closer to her family. Both of Francis's parents have passed away. Francis and Michele have been married and divorced twice. Although they are not married, they remain together as a family, he said.

"We're best of friends," Francis said. "We never had an argument. She's a wonderful woman, but she just has a different view of the world than I do."

Francis's view of the world has not changed all that much from his fun-loving and adventurous days with the 49ers. In 2003, he purchased a 1953 Harley-Davidson Panhead in New Jersey. He decided to ride it back to Nebraska through a snowstorm. A trip that should have taken him about a day and a half, he said, ended up dragging on another full day.

Francis disputes the notion he was a thrill-seeker. He said he always prepared diligently for everything he did, especially his more than 3,500 parachute jumps.

But little can compare to thrill of those glory seasons with the 49ers when he was catching passes from Joe Montana and part of Walsh's intricate game plans.

"My recollections being distant in time and geographical terms, being in San Francisco and playing with the 49ers was sweetness personified," Francis said. "Those guys, fans, coaches, and times were worth a movie, a statue, a time capsule—anything we can do to commemorate and to hold high that unbelievable time in human history. It ranks right up there with the Stone Age as a monumental time in human and earthly history.

"I mean part of that tongue in cheek, but for us who journeyed that time in history, it means that much to us."

JEFF STOVER

Jeff Stover had not played football since high school. Yet he had this funny notion he could play in the NFL.

After the Seattle Seahawks passed on the chance to take a look at this six-foot-five, 275-pound former Olympic hopeful, the 49ers agreed to give him a tryout.

He spent the next seven seasons with the club as a defensive end and ranks 10th on the 49ers' career sacks list with 30.5.

"I was one of those guys who on a whim thought I'd try out and see where it took me," Stover said. "I happened to be in the right place at the right time with the right coaches."

While playing high school football in the farming community of Corning, California, Stover was a one-man wrecking crew. He was the biggest player on the team and also the fastest. He played tailback in the single-wing offense and switched to fullback on pass plays. He also played defensive end and all special teams. He was the punter, place-kicker, and returned punts and kickoffs.

But because Corning wasn't exactly a hotbed for national-caliber talent, nobody knew about his football exploits until he played in a high-school all-star game in Sacramento. Bill Walsh, then the Stanford coach, was in attendance.

Years later, Walsh would remember Stover from what he saw that day.

"He didn't play college football, but he was an outstanding high school player and an all-around great athlete," Walsh said.

Stover had already landed a track scholarship to the University of Oregon because he opened some eyes when he traveled out of the area for meets. As a senior, he was the No. 2-ranked shot putter in the country. Interestingly, he did not even make it to the California State Meet because the top-ranked boy in the state happened to be in the same sparsely populated section. Only the top qualifier earned a trip to the state meet.

After an outstanding career at Oregon, during which time he twice won the Pac-10 Conference title, Stover appeared to be in position to compete for a medal at the 1980 Summer Olympics in Moscow. He had the fourth-best throw in the world at 68 feet, four and a half inches.

"I thought I had a pretty good chance," Stover said.

But Stover never had the opportunity to realize his dream because the United States boycotted the Games. Instead he went to work with his father in the construction business. That was when he had decided to give football another try.

Michael Zagaris photo

JEFF STOVER

Defensive end · Oregon · Ht. 6-5; Wt. 275
Born: May 22, 1958 · 49ers career: 1982-1988

Career highlights: Did not play football in college · World-class competitor in the shot put · Earned roster spot with 49ers in 1982 · Ranks 10th on 49ers' all-time list with 30.5 sacks · Recorded career-high 11 sacks in 1986 · Played 81 games in seven-year career, all with the 49ers.

In need of a door to open, Stover approached Shasta College coach Leon Donahue, who played three seasons for the 49ers as a tackle in the 1960s. Donahue first called the Seahawks, but they were not interested. Then he talked to former teammate Billy Wilson, who worked as a 49ers scout, and got Stover a tryout.

Donahue envisioned Stover as an offensive lineman. He told him to ask for line coach Bobb McKittrick when he arrived for the workout. However, McKittrick was out of the office sick that day. Stover met defensive assistant Bill McPherson.

"He liked what he saw," said Stover, who ran 40 yards in an impressive 4.7 seconds. "He came up to me, put his arm around me and said, 'You're mine.'"

Stover played in all nine games in the strike-shortened 1982 season, but there were plenty of rough times. Because he had not played since high school, he had a lot of learning to do, and teammates and coaches alike often lost their patience with him.

"I got the heck beat out of me," Stover said. "I remember I went to 'Hacksaw' Reynolds and said, 'I'm getting beat up, the players are yelling at me, and the coaches are yelling at me.' And Hacksaw said, 'Hey, man, I've never seen anybody do what you're doing. Keep your mouth shut, keep working hard, and you'll be fine.'"

His third season in the league was expected to be his breakout year. He earned the starting job at defensive end for the regular-season opener against the Detroit Lions. But Stover sustained a potential season-ending tear to the medial collateral ligament in his right knee.

After surgery, team physician Dr. Michael Dillingham told Stover he wanted to use a new technique that might allow him to return to the playing field that season. A typical cast would have kept the knee immobile for six to eight weeks with another six weeks needed to get it back in shape. Stover agreed to serve as a guinea pig, as a hinge was placed in the cast that would allow movement and prevent atrophy from setting in.

Stover returned for the final five games of the regular season, and even played a key role in the 49ers' Super Bowl victory over the Miami Dolphins. He was not officially credited with any tackles, but Stover had a hand in two of the four sacks of Dan Marino.

"I got some hits on him, and I had a blast," Stover said.

Stover put together outstanding seasons in 1985 and 1986, recording 21 sacks during that time. He lined up at defensive end in base situations and often rushed the quarterback as a tackle in passing situations.

He was involved in a controversial play, as he landed hard on Raiders quarterback Jim Plunkett while sacking him in a 1985 game. Plunkett sustained a shoulder injury from which he never recovered, and many accused Stover of a dirty play.

"All week long, we had studied film on people hitting Plunkett, but he was so big and strong that he bounced right off them," Stover said. "We were told to grab him and take him down. I made a move on the guard and came inside and had a straight shot on him. I tried to drive him into the ground, unfortunately someone got hurt.

"It wasn't malicious. I tried to send him letters. He was someone who was an idol of mine, and I respected him. It's too bad it happened, but it's all part of the game."

Stover's career ended after the 1988 season, cut short due to injuries. He has undergone seven surgeries on his right elbow and three on his left—injuries he says were caused because his elbows took the full brunt of the explosion he was able to generate off the snap of the ball.

He lives in Chico, California, where he owns Chico Sports Club, a 70,000-square foot health club that caters to baby boomers and seniors. He has a staff of 130 employees, which has been a challenge to manage. But the best advice Stover received came from his wife, Sharon, with whom he has been married since 1990.

"My wife told me, 'You worked for one of the best-run organizations there was, just look at how Bill Walsh worked with people, and try to duplicate it,'" Stover said.

RIKI
ELLISON

Defense has always been of keen interest to Riki Ellison. In fact, he made it his life's work.

Ellison spent 10 seasons in the NFL, including his first seven with the 49ers, where he was a linebacker on three Super Bowl championship teams.

However, he did not stop rallying support for the defense after his playing days were over. Only now, he is making his mark as founder and president of the Missile Defense Advocacy Alliance, a non-profit organization he founded in 2002 that is based in Alexandria, Virginia.

"It's just my mentality," Ellison said. "But this is not aggressive defense, like a linebacker. It's taken a lot of work to get to the NFL and to get to where I'm at today. I have the same passion for this as I had when I was playing linebacker for the San Francisco 49ers. I'm a cause-related guy. This is a world issue that makes mankind safer. This can help us now and help our children. It's a phenomenal concept and can protect our lives from the most devastating attack known to mankind."

Ellison did not think he was going to get an opportunity for a career in professional football after undergoing three major knee operations at the University of Southern California. In fact, when the Dallas Cowboys flunked him in a pre-draft physical and told him he'd never play in the NFL, he did not bother to attend any of the combines.

However, two days before the 1983 draft, 49ers defensive coaches George Seifert and Bill McPherson went to Los Angeles to see Ellison work out. The team's new strength and conditioning coach, Jerry Attaway, who had come from USC, recommended Ellison to the coaching staff.

"I ended up watching the draft on TV at a friend's house," he said. "Right before ESPN went off the air, I saw my name flash across the screen [in the fifth round]. I wasn't expecting to get drafted."

Ellison started 14 games at left inside linebacker in the 49ers' 3-4 scheme as a rookie. In 1984, he started every game in the 49ers' Super Bowl season that culminated with a 38-16 victory over the Miami Dolphins in Super Bowl XIX at Stanford Stadium in nearby Palo Alto, California.

"That one in San Francisco, playing at home with the fog rolling in and feeling the game was over before we were even introduced was special," Ellison said. "We had that kind of belief in each other. Those couple hours or days, just feeling invincible and hav-

Michael Zagaris photo

RIKI ELLISON

Linebacker · Southern California · Ht. 6-2; Wt. 225
Born: August 15, 1960 · 49ers career: 1983-1988

Career highlights: Selected in fifth round of 1983 draft ·
Earned starting job at left inside linebacker as a rookie, making
NFL All-Rookie team · Led team in tackles (1984 and 1985) ·
Played on two Super Bowl-winning teams · Played 124 games
in nine-year career · Finished career with
Los Angeles Raiders (1990-1992).

ing an inner belief and trust in that group of guys and knowing all the adversity we'd fought through to be the best at what we do for that year. What magical times."

The victory over the Cincinnati Bengals in Super Bowl four years later was also special, as Ellison watched quarterback Joe Montana engineer the game-winning drive in the closing minutes that culminated with his 10-yard touchdown pass to John Taylor.

"I knew we were going to win—we all knew it on the sideline," Ellison said. "The defense did its job, and then we turned the ball over to Joe and the offense."

Ellison was prevented from being on the field for the 49ers' back-to-back Super Bowl titles the next season because of a broken arm. He said he was furious that a team doctor inserted a plate into his broken arm but never took it out, causing the bone to break again. It was about the only way Ellison could be kept off the field during his career.

"Riki is just a driven man," Bill Walsh said. "Anything he takes on, he is going to approach with tremendous intensity."

He played his final three seasons with the Raiders, where he was teammates once again with friends Roger Craig and Ronnie Lott. Ellison retired from football after the 1992 season and moved back to his native New Zealand.

But after a few years he decided it was time to move back to the United States and make a difference. Even during his playing days he would take internships in the offseason with defense and aerospace companies.

Now he has become one of the leading authorities in missile defense, a passion of his since earning a bachelor's degree in international relations in 1983. He also earned an honors certificate in defense and strategic studies from USC, while also playing on a team that won two Rose Bowls and a national championship.

Ellison became interested in the subject upon hearing President Ronald Reagan's speech on missile defense in the spring of 1983. He said the importance of such defense systems is even more urgent since the terror attacks of September 11, 2001.

"I'm speaking on a subject that is important to the country, and it's important to the world and important to the president," Ellison said. "I'm showing the same work ethic and drive and effort as I showed on the football field. It's similar skill sets."

Ellison's organization is non-partisan, and has more than 4,000 members. He said he gave senator John Kerry and President George W. Bush the same information during the 2004 campaign. "I'm a single-issue guy," he said. He took his message to the battleground states leading up to the election.

"My organization represents the United States citizens on this issue," Ellison said. "I go out and listen to the American public, state by state and city by city, and get views on missile defense. I'm also able to educate.

"I take their opinions and make sure we get a system deployed that can protect us against the proliferation of ballistic missiles. My goal is to get a robust, layered defense system in place to protect us against ballistic missiles from any range and any place on the planet."

Ellison said he believes he has already made a difference. He has met with 29 U.S. senators and 26 representatives. He's also met with officials in the White House, National Security Council and Pentagon.

"I've seen candidates change their positions from Howard Dean to Senator Kerry to Wesley Clark," Ellison said. "I've been brought in to brief the White House and then seen missile defense put on the agenda."

Born in New Zealand and of Maori descent, Ellison is a member of the Ngai Tahu, Taranaki, Ngati Ana, and the Ngati Porou Maori tribes. He has been heavily involved in charities and community service. He is the president and founder of Student Athlete Permanent Impact Foundation, a non-profit that helps youths from communities in need through academics and athletics.

He was a volunteer head coach for two seasons at T.C. Williams High School in Alexandria, the inner-city school that was the focal point of the movie *Remember The Titans* before resigning in March 2003.

His "life's work," he says, is to continue to use his knowledge of missile defense to make America safer. And anyone who watched him play football knows what happens when Ellison is determined to accomplish a goal.

"When I played for the 49ers, I was totally focused on the 49ers, because I believed wholeheartedly in what we were doing," he said. "This is the same thing. This is a cause that I'm passionate about."

ROGER CRAIG

R oger Craig was a trend-setter during his 11-year NFL career.
He is the person who coaxed Jerry Rice into a running a particularly demanding hill as part of his training regimen. Now that horse trail off Highway 280 in the Bay Area is commonly referred to as "Jerry's Hill."

It was Craig who became the charter member of the 1,000-1,000 club. Since he gained 1,000 yards rushing and receiving in 1985, only St. Louis Rams running back Marshall Faulk has joined the group.

And Craig was the first player in league history to sign a ceremonial contract so he could retire as a member of an organization with which he was most associated.

"I was the first who did that," Craig said. "I sort of created that whole scenario, and now everybody does it. I think that's great. I got a letter from the league office telling me what a good gesture it was."

Craig spent eight seasons with the 49ers after being selected in the second round of the 1983 draft from Nebraska. He came to epitomize the 49ers' legendary practice habits with his routine of running the length of the field every time he touched the ball.

"Roger's work ethic was stellar," former 49ers coach Bill Walsh said. "His outstanding abilities, combined with his hard work, took him far. A lot of players were just as determined to work as hard as Roger, but they simply could not keep up with him."

The 49ers went to the playoffs in each of Craig's eight seasons with the club. After leaving the 49ers, he also made it to the playoffs with the Los Angeles Raiders and Minnesota Vikings.

But upon the completion of his career, he just didn't feel right retiring with any team other than the 49ers.

"I didn't want to go to another team and retire," Craig said. "I didn't want to retire as a Minnesota Viking. I wanted to retire as a 49er. That's where all my memories were. I did it for the fans. I wanted to come home to where I belong. I appreciated the support the fans gave me, and the organization allowed me to come back."

Craig was especially grateful for the support he received from fans of the 49ers during the most tumultuous time of his career. His fumble late in the 1990 NFC Championship Game was a key play in the New York Giants' 15-13 victory. The next day, he was placed on Plan B, along with Ronnie Lott. Both Craig and Lott ended up signing with the Raiders.

Brad Mangin photo

ROGER CRAIG
Running back · Nebraska · Ht. 6-0; Wt. 225
Born: July 10, 1960 · 49ers career: 1983-1990

Career highlights: Selected in second round of 1983 draft ·
Super Bowl-record three touchdowns in 38-16 victory over
Miami Dolphins in Super Bowl XIX · Named to Pro Bowl four
times · First-team All-Pro in 1985 and 1988 · Became first
player in NFL history to gain 1,000 yards rushing and receiving
in the same season · Len Eshmont Award winner in 1985 and
1988 · Rushed for 8,189 yards and 56 touchdowns on 1,991
career carries · Caught 566 passes for 4,911 yards and 17
touchdowns · Played 165 games in 11-year career · Also
played for Los Angeles Raiders (1991) and Minnesota Vikings
(1992 and 1993) · Retired as a member of 49ers.

"I was already thinking about ways I could redeem myself the following season," Craig said.

But he never got another chance to suit up for the 49ers. However, his official 49ers career ended on a high note several years later.

In August 1994, Craig went to training camp with the 49ers in Rocklin, California, to sign a contract. Owner Eddie DeBartolo and club president Carmen Policy were joined by actor Danny Glover and more than 100 others.

"Throughout my career I received a lot of awards," Craig said that day, alluding to his three Super Bowl rings, four trips to the Pro Bowl and his recognition as 1988 NFL Offensive Player of the Year. "But all of that doesn't compare to coming back to retire as a 49er. It's definitely a dream come true for me."

In the years after Craig retired as a member of the 49ers organization, such players as Eugene Lockhart (Dallas), Art Monk (Washington) and Leonard Marshall (New York Giants) did the same thing.

In the early months of 2005, Dallas running back Emmitt Smith returned to the Cowboys in a ceremonial role, and return man Brian Mitchell retired as a member of the Washington Redskins. Of course, former 49ers receiver Jerry Rice had made his plans known since he left the organization in 2001 to retire as a member of the 49ers, too.

Craig was a virtual unknown when the 49ers went to the Super Bowl in January 1985. But he made his mark on the game's biggest stage. Craig scored a Super Bowl-record three touchdowns, getting into the end zone on eight- and 16-yard passes from Joe Montana, and a two-yard touchdown run. He also high-stepped his way onto the cover of *Sports Illustrated*, with the headline reading, "Roger Craig Hammers the Dolphins."

At a ring ceremony that offseason, Walsh pulled Craig aside and told him he expected 1,000 yards out of him the following season. Craig says he wasn't sure whether Walsh meant 1,000 yards rushing or receiving. So he didn't leave any room for error.

Although he was the team's fullback, with Wendell Tyler as the halfback, Craig led the team in rushing yards (1,050) and receiving (92 catches for 1,016 yards). Faulk became the second member of the 1,000-1,000 fraternity in 1999 when he rushed for 1,381 yards and caught 1,048 yards worth of passes. He was voted NFL Offensive Player of the Year.

In 2002, Charlie Garner, then of the Oakland Raiders, came tantalizingly close to joining the exclusive club. He rushed for 962 yards and caught 941 yards in passes. Craig said he was upset Garner did not get it.

"He was so close in both categories," Craig said. "But he didn't get a chance. I was upset they didn't feature him more. I want to see more of these younger guys take pride in being a complete back. I want more players to do it, because I'm the godfather of the group."

Craig still ranks as the 49ers' No. 2 all-time rusher with 7,064 yards, and is No. 3 all-time with 508 receptions. It's been more than a decade since his NFL career came to an end, but Roger Craig is still running.

The tireless fitness buff started running marathons in 2004 at the age of 43. Initially, Craig's goal was to run five marathons in his life. His oldest sister, Brenda Martinez, completed five marathons before she died in a car accident seven years earlier. In his first marathon in San Diego, Craig endured a debilitating case of cramps and struggled to finish in four hours and nine minutes.

"She kept me going," Craig said. "I kept saying, 'I'm doing this for you, Brenda.'"

He subsequently ran marathons in Chicago (three hours, 53 minutes) and in Arizona (three hours, 49 minutes). His goal is to qualify for the Boston Marathon in August 2006. He will need to shave 19 minutes off his time to reach what he calls, "the Super Bowl of marathons."

It was a busy year for Craig, who also released his second book, *Roger Craig's Tales from the San Francisco 49ers Sideline.* He also works full-time as

Roger Craig is successful in his post-football career while also remaining in good enough physical condition to regularly run marathons.
Photo courtesy of Dan Audick

director of business development for TIBCO Software. Craig's duties include marketing, creating new business, helping the sales team, closing deals, as well as work with human resources in the interviewing of prospective employees.

He and his wife, Vernessia, have three daughters and two sons. His oldest son, Rogdrick, redshirted in the 2004-2005 season after earning a basketball scholarship to Pepperdine. Daughter Rometra, who played basketball at Southern California, is playing in Europe, while his oldest daughter, Damesha, was a track standout at UCLA.

RENALDO NEHEMIAH

R enaldo Nehemiah eschewed team sports in college, in part, because of the politics involved, he says.

In an individual sports such as track and field, it was all about talent. The person who ran the fastest was the winner. That kind of objectivity appealed to Nehemiah.

However, Nehemiah's rationale was not foolproof. The darkest time in his athletic career was in 1980 when politics was the reason the United States boycotted the Summer Olympics in Moscow.

In 1982, with no Olympic gold medal to his credit, his profile as the world's best hurdler was heightened because he decided to play a team sport—signing a four-year, $500,000 contract with the 49ers as a wide receiver.

"Unfortunately, I had to play professional football to get my just due as a great athlete," Nehemiah said. "In Europe, I was an international celebrity. In the United States, I was vindicated once I played America's game of football."

Nehemiah played three seasons with the 49ers, catching 43 passes for 754 yards and four touchdowns. His fourth year was spent on injured reserve with a back injury.

"I played out my four years, and it was time to renegotiate," Nehemiah said. "I had all this talent that I had given up on in track and field, and I wasn't a full-time player in football. I didn't want to waste the talent I was blessed with by watching from the sideline."

Also, Nehemiah had already spent a large sum of money during a four-and-a-half-year legal battle with track's U.S. and international governing bodies, which ruled he could not compete because he was a professional. In 1986, the ban was lifted when track changed its rules. He returned to the hurdles and achieved world rankings four times from 1988 to 1991, but was never able to regain what he lost when he decided to give the NFL a try.

"I don't know how you can put on 22 pounds and not have it hurt you," Nehemiah said. "Plus, I was getting out of shape when I was on the sideline. It's a different type of training. When you don't use your world-class speed on a consistent basis, it goes dormant. I lost a lot of flexibility by just standing around on the sideline and then in a moment's notice going out and running in a game."

Nehemiah did not play football at the University of Maryland, where he established himself as one of track's biggest international superstars. From 1978 to 1981, Nehemiah was the world's premier hurdler. He became the first person to break 13 seconds in the

RENALDO NEHEMIAH
Wide receiver · Maryland · Ht. 6-1; Wt. 177
Born: May 24, 1959 · 49ers career: 1982-1984

Career highlights: Did not play football in college · World-class hurdler · Set world record in 110-meter high hurdles in 1981 · Signed with 49ers in 1982 · Caught 43 passes for 754 yards in career · Played in 49ers' 1984 Super Bowl victory · Played 40 games in three-year career.

110-meter high hurdles, posting a world-record time of 12.93 in 1981. He was inducted into the National Track and Field Hall of Fame in 1997.

The 49ers won their first Super Bowl in 1981, and wide receiver Dwight Clark took part in the popular "Superstars" competition that was televised on ABC. Nehemiah blew away a field that consisted of the top athletes in every sport. (He ultimately won the competition four times.)

"Dwight Clark told me that he thought I was a phenomenal talent, and that Bill Walsh would love a guy like me," Nehemiah said. "Bill was intrigued. Once word got out that I tried out with the 49ers, I could've picked where I wanted to go."

Nehemiah appeared on the cover of *Sports Illustrated* on April 26, 1982, wearing a 49ers' No. 83 jersey, football in his arm, while clearing a hurdle. The headline blared, "Hurdling Into The NFL."

When Nehemiah reported to the 49ers, he weighed 169 pounds. The 49ers did not want his playing weight to dip below 185 pounds, which undoubtedly slowed him down a little. Still, his speed created some problems even for one of the great quarterbacks of all time.

"I remember one of the things Joe [Montana] said to me was, 'It looks like you're not even running, but when I throw you the ball, I underthrow you,'" Nehemiah said. "I told him that it's a different kind of efficiency that a track runner uses."

Even Nehemiah's speed could not prevent him from absorbing the kind of viscous hit that made his coach rethink how to use him.

In a 1983 game against the Atlanta Falcons, Nehemiah was flattened when defensive back Kenny Johnson knocked him out on a hit over the middle. Nehemiah's fumble was returned 64 yards for a touchdown. Nehemiah sustained a serious concussion, but the gruesome hit had much more of an impact on Walsh than on Nehemiah, he said.

"My football career was going along fairly well until I got knocked out," Nehemiah said. "That's when Bill became more of a surrogate father than a coach. He became pretty protective of me. Bill didn't want to have me exposed like that again. I was catching the ball over the middle and was laid out, so they started keeping me on the outside or have me running deep routes down the middle so there'd be less a chance of that happening. Because not every situation calls for those kinds of routes, my opportunities to be effective were limited.

"I didn't understand it at the time. But I think Bill knew all eyes were going to be on me. Maybe he didn't want to be the one who, some might say, got the world's greatest hurdler maimed."

Nehemiah, who was tagged with the nickname "Noodles" upon joining the club because some teammates thought he lacked physical toughness, earned a great deal of respect when he returned to action the following week. He played in every game his first three seasons in the league.

Nehemiah earned one Super Bowl ring with the 49ers, as he received extensive playing time in the 49ers' 38-16 victory over the Miami Dolphins in Super Bowl XIX. Although Nehemiah did not have a catch in the game, he is proud that some of his deep routes helped open up underneath passes for Clark and running back Roger Craig.

The Super Bowl ended up being Nehemiah's Olympics. The boycott in 1980 likely cost him a gold medal, and he was a broadcaster during the 1984 Olympics in Los Angeles.

"I was clearly the best hurdler in 1980, and not getting a chance to go to the Olympics was very hurtful to me," he said. "It took me many, many years to address it. That was the single biggest motivating factor in going into football."

Upon retiring from track and field, Nehemiah put his brokerage license to work in helping athletes. In 1997, he became an agent for Gold Medal Management. Now, he is one of the most influential agents in the business with the athletic representation firm of Octagon. In 2005, he began his sixth year as Octagon's director of track and field world-wide, with a client list that includes Allyson Felix, Justin Gatlin and Obadele Thompson.

Nehemiah says he still sees a lot of his former 49ers teammates from time to time, including Ronnie Lott, Craig, Mike Wilson, Joe Montana, Jim Stuckey, and Randy Cross.

"I was a world-record holder, and I have a Super Bowl ring," Nehemiah said. "There are very few people who can say that. I played for the best team ever during that time. It's an experience I'd never take back."

JOHN FRANK

When tight end John Frank informed 49ers vice president Bill Walsh of his decision, he was met with neither anger nor a blank stare. No, Walsh broke into a laugh when Frank broke the news he was retiring at age 27 after five NFL seasons.

"He thought I was joking," Frank said.

In the prime of his football career, and just a couple months after being the starting tight end on the 49ers' Super Bowl champion, Frank decided to pursue another line of work. He went back to medical school.

It was a decision Frank said he never regretted. But in recent years he has gotten involved again in athletics.

While working as one of the nation's top hair transplant specialists in New York, Frank helped create the Israeli bobsled team. His goal is for the two-man bobsled team to qualify for the 2006 Winter Olympics in Turin, Italy.

Even if the team makes the Olympics, it is unlikely Frank will be shooting down the frozen track. Frank will be nearing his 44th birthday, and he would like for youngster Moshe Horowitz to take his place full time as the brakeman on the sled.

"I'm happy to turn the reins over and try to get the new blood in there," Frank said. "I almost feel out of place in some ways. I'm so much older and I've only been bobsledding a couple years. I derive equal satisfaction from seeing the team do well, whether I'm in there or not."

Frank has always been a team player. The only negative aspect of walking away from the 49ers, he said, was the feeling he might be leaving the club in a bad spot. After all, it was unclear at the time if they had anyone capable of replacing him on the roster.

Walsh once called Frank "probably the most underrated of any player we ever had." Hall of Fame defensive end Howie Long said of Frank: "He's like a pit bull who is always attacking you." In his rookie season, Frank got in a memorable scuffle with New York Giants outside linebacker Lawrence Taylor, and earned a spot on the "All-Madden Team" for his tenacity.

Without Frank on the 49ers in 1989, the team still repeated as Super Bowl champions.

"They had a hard time the next year without me," Frank quipped.

He said it was a relief to see the 49ers remain as the league's best team, because he did not want to be responsible if the team had struggled.

JOHN FRANK

Tight end · Ohio State · Ht. 6-3; Wt. 225
Born: April 17, 1962 · 49ers career: 1984-1988

Career highlights: Selected in second round of 1984 draft ·
Played on two Super Bowl- winning teams, including one as a
starter · Caught 65 passes for 662 yards and 10 touchdowns in
his career · Played 66 games in his five-year
career, all with the 49ers.

"I'm really glad," he said. "I never wanted to pull a Ricky Williams. I didn't want that on my resume. At that time I didn't realize, I guess, how important it was that I was so up front with the team."

Frank met with Walsh several weeks prior to the 1989 draft and suggested the team select a tight end in the first couple rounds. They did, choosing Wesley Walls in the second round. Although Walls went on to have a fine career elsewhere in the league, injuries limited his effectiveness with the 49ers.

"As amazing as Brent Jones turned out to be, they didn't know at the time how good he was going to be," Frank said. "So it was a big concern."

Frank earned $357,000 during the 1988 season, and it was widely speculated he was using medical school as a negotiating ploy to bargain for a bigger contract.

What is not as widely known is that Frank had planned to leave the game the previous season. He became the starting tight end late in the strike-marred 1987 season, and he told his mother he was going to medical school full time in 1988.

"The only person I really told was my mom, who didn't want me to play football in the first place a million years ago," Frank said. "I thought she'd be happy. She said, 'Why? You just made the starting team. Give it one more year. Do it for yourself.'"

It turned out to be the best advice Frank could have received. He started in Super Bowl XXIII against the Cincinnati Bengals. Frank caught two passes for 15 yards in the game, and was on the field for a good portion of the 49ers' winning drive. He remembers things a little differently than the commonly held belief.

"Everybody talks about how poised Joe was during the drive," Frank said, "but I'm not so sure he was as poised as he was made out to be. He was hyperventilating. But it was pretty amazing how it just clicked. That stands out."

What also stands out is Frank's overzealous celebration in the locker room. Frank gave owner Eddie DeBartolo such a robust hug that the boss's head whipped back into a locker, leaving a nasty gash. "That was my last hit in the NFL," Frank said.

His decision to leave the game was reinforced in his final season when he sustained a broken left hand that required five pins. He also knew his supple hands could be put to much better use holding a scalpel than catching footballs.

"I wanted to finish what I started, which was medical school," Frank said. "There was nothing that would get in my way of finishing school."

Frank worked in head and neck surgery during his residency. He then went into facial plastic and reconstructive surgery, with a practice in San Francisco from 2000 to 2003. He left to become Medical Hair Restoration's lead surgeon at its office in Manhattan. On this particular day, Frank consulted with a young lady from the Dominican Republic who had been completely bald since childhood.

He said he performs more surgeries of this kind than any doctor in the United States, if not the world. Yet he also creates time for his quest to land a bobsled team in the Olympics.

Frank and his friend, Aaron Zeff of San Francisco, hatched the idea while on a ski lift in Tahoe in 2001. Both men are American-born Jews who have since earned their Israeli citizenship.

Frank did some medical training in Israel, and both men have been to the country several times to get authorization to spearhead the bobsled team. In the spring of 2004, they held tryouts in Tel Aviv, where Horowitz joined the mix.

The Israeli team—or the "Chosen Frozen," as they've been dubbed—will have to rank in the top 28 in the 2005-2006 World Cup season to qualify for a spot in the Olympics. In their first two seasons of competition, the team had yet to establish itself among the top 30 teams in the world.

"It's going to be tough," Frank said. "The first year we were awfully proud to be there. The second year we made some real strides, but we got our butts kicked [at the World Cup]. Maybe that was a good eye-opener for us. It's going to take a lot more athleticism, financing, and dedication to be medal contenders."

JEFF FULLER

Jeff Fuller has never watched a replay, nor does he have any desire to ever see the play that ended his football career.

Fuller had emerged into a top-flight safety for the 49ers in 1989 when he sustained a serious neck injury, forever changing his life.

While making a tackle against the New England Patriots, Fuller absorbed a violent impact that tore his C-5, C-6 and C-7 vertebrae out of his spine. Initially he had limited movement of his arms and legs.

"Everything pretty much came back in a day or two, except for my right arm," Fuller said. "For a while you'll think you're getting ready to turn the corner and it'll be better, but I've adjusted. It's been quite a while; you learn to adapt.

"I'm a lot better than I thought I'd be. It could've been a lot worse."

A decade and a half later, Fuller still has paralysis in his right arm and elbow, and the movements in his wrist and hand are restricted.

"I can run; I can do just about everything," Fuller said. "I don't play basketball or golf, but I'm able to do almost everything without being held back."

Fuller is not one to sit around and feel sorry for himself. Although he admits he endured some difficult times because of the injury, Fuller says there are many positives that came out of the unfortunate play.

"In a lot of ways, it made me a better person. It made me a more stable person," said Fuller, who experienced some off-the-field problems during his time with the 49ers. "I have a family now and I'm settled. At that time, I wasn't settled. I wasn't even thinking along those lines. But it's tough to have a serious injury like that. It would've been nice to play the sport and have success and come out of it without the injury."

Fuller and his wife, Leslie, whom he had dated the two years prior to the injury, got married and had four children. The ordeal solidified their bond.

"My wife stood by me through all of that," he said. "As a matter of fact, she was my biggest supporter. After an injury like this, you're not around the team as much. You're on your own a lot of the time, and there were some lonely times when I was going through physical therapy."

Fuller underwent five surgeries, including a nerve graft at Stanford Hospital, where he was taken immediately after the incident. In a lucky twist, the 49ers played that game at Stanford Stadium because the Loma Prieta earthquake five days earlier had damaged Candlestick Park.

Michael Zagaris photo

JEFF FULLER
Safety · Texas A&M · Ht. 6-2; Wt. 216
Born: August 8, 1962 · 49ers career: 1984-1989

**Career highlights: Selected in fifth round of 1984 draft ·
Moved into starting lineup at strong safety in 1987 · Named
second-team All-NFL in 1987 · Recorded 10 career interceptions · Played 72 games in six-year career.**

"That was the best thing for me, because the [medical] facility was right there on campus," Fuller said. "If I had been somewhere like Candlestick, it would've been a lot more difficult."

That whole week leading up to the game was out of the ordinary. Fuller, Tom Rathman, John Taylor and Daniel Stubbs had planned to go to the Giants-Athletics World Series game. They were still at Fuller's house playing cards when the earthquake hit.

Fuller lived on the same street as Roger Craig, Pete Kugler, and Dwight Hicks, and nobody knew whether the team was practicing the next day. When they were informed that practices would be held like normal, several players loaded into Eric Wright's car.

"Every time we got to an overpass or a bridge, Eric Wright would gun it," Fuller said. "After a while, we were like, 'What are you doing?' And he said, 'I'm not going to let a bridge fall on us.'"

Fuller found a home with the 49ers after coming to the team as a fifth-round draft pick in 1984. It was a daunting task as a rookie to try to earn some playing time in a secondary that featured four stars: Ronnie Lott, Dwight Hicks, Eric Wright, and Carlton Williamson.

"It was a tough place to play because all of those guys were Pro Bowlers," Fuller said. "Breaking into that lineup was going to be pretty tough. But thankfully, Ray Rhodes [defensive backs coach] and George Seifert [defensive coordinator] found a place for me. I played quite a bit my rookie year."

Fuller was used as the team's fifth defensive back, though he played linebacker his last two seasons at Texas A&M. In the 49ers' Super Bowl XIX victory over the Miami Dolphins, Fuller had four tackles and broke up a pass in a 38-16 victory.

In 1987 and 1988, he started 26 games at strong safety. He started in Super Bowl XXIII and had five tackles and a pass defensed in the 49ers' 20-16 victory over the Cincinnati Bengals. Fuller did his part to hold running back Ickey Woods to 79 yards on 20 rushing attempts.

"We kept him from doing his shuffle in the end zone," Fuller says proudly.

After that season, Fuller earned a sizable contract extension after a holdout through most of training camp. Getting a big-money deal made him all the more determined to prove he was worth the hefty bump in salary, he said.

However, on the third play of the 49ers' seventh game of the season, October 22, his life changed.

Patriots running back John Stephens took a pitch and ran a sweep to the right side of the field. Fuller came up at full speed and delivered a hit that produced a sickening thud.

"When I hit him, it was like sticking a finger in a wall socket," Fuller said. "Everything short-circuited."

Fuller never lost consciousness. He said everything slowed down for the 15 minutes he remained motionless on the field before being taken out of the stadium in an ambulance. He heard what his teammates were saying; he was able to pick out individual voices from the crowd of 70,000.

"I felt calm," Fuller said. "More than anything, I was cautious. I stressed to them that I couldn't move."

Following the injury, Fuller received many uplifting cards and letters. Stephens wrote to him, as did former New England receiver Darryl Stingley, who was paralyzed in a 1978 preseason game against the Oakland Raiders.

Fuller is grateful for the rapport he developed with owner Eddie DeBartolo and head coach Bill Walsh. Fuller and DeBartolo both contributed to an annuity to make sure Fuller would have money for the rest of his life, he said.

In 2003 when Ronnie Lott had his jersey retired during a halftime ceremony of a game in San Francisco, DeBartolo picked Fuller up in his private jet to be part of the festivities. Fuller said he also speaks with Walsh at least once a month.

"When I look back, it was a great career," Fuller said. "And what made it such a special part of my life was having so many great friends. One of the best friends I got out of playing with the 49ers is Bill Walsh. He's a wonderful guy and very instrumental in making my career what it was."

Fuller's opinion of the sport of football has not changed. It is still a large part of his life. He coached at a private high school in Charlotte, North Carolina. He then joined head coach Doug Williams's staff at Morehouse College in Atlanta for one season before Williams went on to succeed Eddie Robinson at Grambling State. Fuller decided to return to his hometown of Dallas, rather than make the move to Louisiana.

Now he manages some real-estate investments and thoroughly enjoys the family life. He has a high-school age boy and three girls. His son, Jeff Jr., is a standout football and basketball player.

"We don't have any pictures of the 49ers on the wall or anything like that," Fuller said. "It's mainly because that's part of my life that is in the past. My daughter talked about the injury with me once, but it made her sad.

"We don't watch any tapes related to it. It happened, and I'm moving forward."

GUY McINTYRE

G uy McIntyre certainly made a strong contribution to the 49ers' dominance during his five-time Pro Bowl career. But he also made a contribution to pop culture.

After all, William "The Refrigerator" Perry owes everything to the former 49ers guard.

Coach Bill Walsh had an ingenious idea during the 1984 season. His starting backfield consisted of halfback Wendell Tyler and fullback Roger Craig. Craig was a determined blocker, but sometimes his 225-pound frame was no match for the behemoths who lined up at defensive tackle.

Walsh had the inspiration to use McIntyre as a blocking back in short-yardage situations. He used the "Angus" personnel group against the Chicago Bears in the 1984 NFC Championship Game.

Meanwhile, Bears head coach Mike Ditka seethed on the sideline during the 49ers' 23-0 victory. The next season, Ditka used "The Fridge" in that same role against the 49ers as a form of revenge. It became a national sensation when Perry scored a touchdown against the Green Bay Packers in a game on *Monday Night Football*.

Perry also scored a touchdown in Super Bowl XX, as Ditka gave him the ball on the goal line instead of Walter Payton.

"I never got the ball," McIntyre said, "so I never got a touchdown or the McDonald's commercials. But I also didn't have 'The Fridge's' smile and his girth. He ended up making a lot of money off me, and I never asked for a commission."

Walsh said he utilized McIntyre in the backfield because of the qualities he saw in him as a guard.

"He was just a fine all-around athlete," Walsh said. "He was probably the best all-around guard we had. He could pull and trap and move. That's why we used him in the backfield. I wish I would've done more of that."

McIntyre had to wait his turn to break into the starting lineup, as the 49ers' offensive line featured such stalwarts as guards John Ayers and Randy Cross, and center Fred Quillan.

Finally, after more than four seasons of waiting his turn, McIntyre saw increased playing time in 1988, starting 12 games. In 1989, he started 14 games at left guard and was named to his NFC Pro Bowl team. The 49ers won Super Bowl titles in '88 and '89.

"Doing it back-to-back was special," McIntyre said, "so that second one in 1989 is the one that really stands out. Also, that was the first year I went to the Pro Bowl. After you win the Super Bowl and you reach the pinnacle, you go back to Square One for the next

Michael Zagaris photo

GUY McINTYRE

Offensive guard · Georgia · Ht. 6-3; Wt. 268
Born: February 17, 1961 · 49ers career: 1984-1993

**Career highlights: Selected in third round of 1984 draft ·
Played on three 49ers Super Bowl-winning teams · Selected to
Pro Bowl in five consecutive seasons (1989-1993) · First-team
All-NFL in 1989, 1992 and 1993 · Bobb McKittrick Award
winner in 1990 and 1992 · Played 187 games in 13-year NFL
career · Also played for Green Bay Packers (1994) and
Philadelphia Eagles (1995-1996).**

Guy McIntyre regrets leaving the 49ers in 1994 but is back as director of player development.
Photo courtesy of Dan Audick

season. Then to get back there through all the adversity and all the things that can happen is really an accomplishment.

"On top of what team accomplishment, to also be rewarded with a trip to the Pro Bowl made that extremely memorable. Not only was I on the best team, but I was also considered one of the best players at my position."

McIntyre was the prototype for the 49ers' style of line play. Offensive line coach Bobb McKittrick preferred smaller, athletic players over the big, lumbering types. When McIntyre accepted a scholarship to the University of Georgia, he reported to school as a 225-pound tight end.

But because future NFL draft picks Clarence Kay and Norris Brown were already at tight end, McIntyre had to find somewhere else to play. He played some defense in his first season, then switched back to tight end during summer camp at Georgia.

When it was suggested he might be groomed to become the eventual replacement at center for Ray Donaldson, who enjoyed a lengthy professional career, McIntyre was not pleased. Eventually, the thought of becoming a full-time offensive lineman became easier to take.

In his final two seasons at Georgia, his line coach was Alex Gibbs, who later became famous for his work with the Denver Broncos' Super Bowl teams. With the 49ers, McIntyre was under the tutelage of McKittrick. Gibbs and McKittrick are considered two of the best line coaches in NFL history.

McIntyre had a back problem his sophomore season, and the injury was disclosed leading up to the draft. He had a narrowing of a vertebra in his back, a condition that might have led some teams to drop him down their draft boards. The 49ers selected him in the third round of the 1984 draft.

"There was a reason why he was still available for us," Walsh said. "There was some gamble in drafting him."

One of the most tumultuous times in McIntyre's career came during the 1987 strike, which saw the cancellation of one game. Although many of the big-name 49ers were loyal to owner Eddie DeBartolo, there was no question where McIntyre came down on the issue. His mother got fired from her job at a meat production factory in Thomasville, Georgia, because of her union ties, McIntyre said.

"It was a lesson," McIntyre said. "I've always been a strong proponent of unions because of that situation. What happened to my mom was that she tried to make the working conditions better for herself and her co-workers and make life conditions better for her children."

McIntyre's mother eventually went back to school, and now she works as an assistant to the anesthesiologist at a Thomasville hospital.

His career with the 49ers came to an early end after the 1993 season when he turned down the 49ers' offer. He signed with the Green Bay Packers, where he lasted just one season before finishing his career with two years in Philadelphia.

"I felt different about what they wanted to pay me," McIntyre said. "I got a little bold and brash, and things didn't turn out the way I thought they would."

McIntyre, who was entering his 11th year in the league, was seen as a player for the 49ers' system, he says. His availability on the market also came at a time when the league was seeking 300-pounders to play the guard positions.

"I apologized to Mr. DeBartolo [several years later]," McIntyre said. "He had invested a lot in me, and I was grateful that he gave me an opportunity to prove myself and support my family."

McIntyre rejoined the 49ers after his career was completed. Now, he works as the team's director of player development, a position he has held since the fall of 2003. In his capacity with the 49ers, he works with players in career transition, life skills and family assistance.

"These players have to come to realize that even if they last 20 years in the game, which, of course, very few players will, they're still going to be young when they retire and they're going to want to do something with their lives," McIntyre said.

TOM RATHMAN

Tom Rathman's home in the Bay Area remains empty during the fall. He bought the house in the mid-1980s, and has no intention of selling it, because he plans on returning some day.

In a perfect world, Rathman never would have moved away in the first place. He never would have left the 49ers to play one season with the Los Angeles Raiders. And he certainly never would have been forced to leave the 49ers' coaching staff to follow coach Steve Mariucci to the Detroit Lions.

"I come back every month in the offseason, but during the season I don't get a chance to come back," Rathman said. "I'm doing some work on the house, so it'll be organized and in good shape when we move back."

And how long will that be?

"Not as long as I'm coaching in Detroit," he said.

Rathman had always signed one-year contracts since joining the 49ers' coaching staff full-time late in the 1996 season. But he had already made a commitment to stay with the Lions in 2005 when he thought it was clear the 49ers would not be making any front-office changes for a while.

Although Rathman was diplomatic, it was clear he felt then-49ers general manager Terry Donahue was the reason he was not retained on head coach Dennis Erickson's staff after Mariucci was fired.

"It goes deeper than Dennis," Rathman said. "That's my opinion. I've known John York for a long time, and I don't think John had anything to do with it. It was a simple fact that the people running the organization wanted to go in a different direction and get away from the 49ers tradition."

The 49ers' last tie to the grand tradition of the 1980s disappeared when Rathman was not retained, forcing him to accept Mariucci's offer to serve as running backs coach of the Detroit Lions.

Rathman was one of the players who epitomized the 49ers during their decade of dominance. Rathman was a fullback when the position was an integral part of the team's fabled "West Coast Offense." In eight seasons, he rushed for 1,902 yards in the regular season and another 287 in the playoffs. He also caught 294 passes, including a career-high 73 in 1989.

Brad Mangin photo

TOM RATHMAN

Fullback · Nebraska · Ht. 6-1; Wt. 232
Born: October 7, 1962 · 49ers career: 1986-1993

Career highlights: Selected in third round of 1986 draft ·
Earned starting job at fullback in 1987 · Gained 2,020 yards
rushing and 26 touchdowns on 544 carries in career · Caught
320 passes for 2,684 yards and eight touchdowns · Played 131
games in nine-year career · Finished career with
Los Angeles Raiders (1994).

Rathman certainly knew what to do with the football in his hands, but his biggest contribution came as a blocker. He helped clear the path for halfback Roger Craig, as well as protecting quarterback Joe Montana from the dangers of blitzing linebackers.

"I was kind of an extension of the offensive line," Rathman said, "so I knew who to block and who the line was going to block."

Rathman and Craig, both of whom went to the University of Nebraska, were virtually interchangeable parts in the backfield. Because they had just a good rapport on the field, there were times when they would switch positions without the coaching staff knowing.

Their familiarity with each other benefited the 49ers immeasurably during their time together. But it also almost backfired in the closing minute of Super Bowl XXIII at Joe Robbie Stadium in Miami.

With 39 seconds remaining and the 49ers trailing 16-13 with the ball on the Cincinnati Bengals' 10-yard line, Rathman and Craig lined up in the wrong positions and executed the wrong responsibilities. However, disaster was avoided when Montana quickly delivered an on-target pass to receiver John Taylor, the second option on the play behind Craig.

"If you look at it, what happened was that it [the mix-up in the backfield] created a window for Joe to throw the ball," Rathman said of the game-winning touchdown pass in the 49ers' 20-16 victory.

As exciting as it was to win the Super Bowl in the final minute, Rathman said the most memorable victory during his career was the 49ers' 28-3 whipping of the Chicago Bears two weeks earlier in the NFC Championship Game. The game was played in wind chill of minus-26 degrees at Soldier Field.

"That game stands out because we were able to go into that atmosphere and dominate," he said. "There was no question who was going to win it."

Another game for Rathman stands out for an entirely different reason. In the fourth week of the 1989 season, the 49ers held a 12-10 lead over the Los Angeles Rams in the fourth quarter when Rathman fumbled for only the second time in four seasons. The Rams drove 72 yards in the closing minutes for the winning field goal. Even after all these years, Rathman is unable to erase that memory.

"We lost only two games that season," Rathman said. "Whenever a player is the reason for a loss, you remember it. In my house, we call that day 'Black Sunday.'"

Rathman certainly had a lot more highs than lows during his 49ers career. In 1994, he played for the Raiders. As luck would have it, his first game in the silver and black was against the 49ers at Candlestick Park.

He retired at the end of the season and had a chance to return to the 49ers in 1995 when several fullbacks, including starter William Floyd, went down with season-ending injuries.

"George Seifert called and asked if I wanted to come back," Rathman said. "I went down to talk to them and they talked to my agent, Marvin Demoff. It was almost a done deal. But then I thought, 'I'm not going to do it.' I didn't feel like I was able to play up to that standard."

In all likelihood, Rathman would have been on the field for the first play of the 49ers' NFC Divisional playoff game against the Green Bay Packers. A swing pass that would have gone his way instead went to Adam Walker, playing with a broken thumb.

Walker caught Steve Young's pass but then fumbled. Green Bay's Craig Newsome picked up the ball and ran 31 yards for a touchdown. The Packers rode that momentum to a 27-17 upset victory.

Meanwhile, Rathman was already beginning his coaching career at San Mateo's Serra High School, the alma mater of New England quarterback Tom Brady, Hall of Fame receiver Lynn Swann and baseball's Barry Bonds. The next year, Rathman served as head coach Doug Cosbie's offensive coordinator at NCAA Division III school Menlo College.

After the college season, he joined the 49ers' staff full time. Mariucci hired him as running backs coach at the start of the 1997 season.

Rathman has not ruled out the possibility of being a head coach at some point in his career, but he knows the first step is to become an offensive coordinator. He spoke with new 49ers coach Mike Nolan in January 2005 about a position on the 49ers' staff, but the Lions were not going to let him out of his contract.

He admits it was difficult for him to move his wife, Holly, and their three daughters to Michigan in 2003 and leave the organization he helped win two Super Bowls.

"I consider myself a 49er," Rathman said. "I'll always consider myself a 49er. As a player and a coach, I was willing to do whatever I had to do to make the organization successful. That was my mentality. I didn't want to leave, but you have to go where the opportunities are."

JIM DRUCKENMILLER

During the 1997 NFL Draft, the 49ers were in the market for a quarterback. General manager Dwight Clark enlisted the help of quarterback guru Bill Walsh to look at the top players available.

From there, the facts get a little hazy. This is what is known: The 49ers selected the player who was universally seen as the top-rated quarterback available.

The 49ers drafted strong-armed Jim Druckenmiller of Virginia Tech with the No. 26 overall pick. If everything had turned out as planned, Druckenmiller might still be the 49ers' quarterback. Instead, his tenure with the team lasted just two seasons.

Druckenmiller saw limited action as a rookie, starting an early-season game on the road against the St. Louis Rams, which the 49ers won. He did not attempt a pass in the NFL after his first year in the league.

Walsh, who succeeded Clark as general manager, would later ridicule the decision to select Druckenmiller instead of Jake Plummer, whom the Arizona Cardinals drafted 16 spots later. Although Walsh was known to be enamored of Plummer, he also compared Druckenmiller to Drew Bledsoe in a story that appeared in *USA Today* prior to the draft. "I don't see anybody in his category," Walsh was quoted as saying.

Clark said Walsh had told him in meetings that Druckenmiller was the most talented quarterback in the draft, but Plummer fit the 49ers' system better. Druckenmiller understands that assessment. He said he realizes his best chance at a successful professional career was not with the 49ers.

"I think I could've made it, but I don't think the 49ers would've been the exact fit for me," Druckenmiller said. "I would've been more of a fit with a team like Pittsburgh that uses play-action and a running game. I don't know about a West Coast offense for my style."

Druckenmiller was brought to the 49ers to become Steve Young's heir to the team's quarterback throne. But after two seasons with the club, Dwight Clark had moved on to the Cleveland Browns, and Walsh was in charge of personnel. Walsh did not seem to have much tolerance for Druckenmiller's antics.

Some thought Druckenmiller lacked the maturity the organization sought from its quarterback. During his rookie season with the 49ers, Druckenmiller rode his motorcycle onto the set of a television show, and he missed a team flight to Atlanta, forcing him to pay his own way on a red-eye to join his teammates.

JIM DRUCKENMILLER

Quarterback · Virginia Tech · Ht. 6-5; Wt. 230
Born: September 19, 1972 · 49ers career: 1997-1998

Career highlights: Selected in first round (26th overall) of 1997
draft · Only NFL start came in second game of rookie season,
a 15-12 victory over the St. Louis Rams · Traded to Miami
Dolphins in 1999 · Played in eight
games in three-year NFL career.

In the spring of 1999, Walsh asked Druckenmiller to play in NFL Europe. Druckenmiller declined because he did not want to risk an injury, and he suspected he was not going to fit into Walsh's plans anyway.

"Bill wanted me to go, and when I didn't, I became a bit of an outcast," Druckenmiller said. "That's something I might reconsider now. Maybe if I had to do it over again, I would go to Europe, because that would have given me an opportunity to be seen on film."

Further complicating Druckenmiller's future with the club, he was brought up on rape charges that spring. Although he was cleared of any wrongdoing after jury deliberations lasted just 45 minutes, Druckenmiller's image had taken a hit.

The 49ers traded Druckenmiller to the Miami Dolphins for two seventh-round picks, which turned out to be Pro Bowl long-snapper Brian Jennings and pass-catching tight end Eric Johnson.

Druckenmiller thought the move to Miami might be the break he needed because head coach Jimmy Johnson had considered drafting Druckenmiller with the No. 15 overall pick in 1997 but opted for University of Miami (Florida) receiver Yatil Green instead. But Druckenmiller lasted just one year in Miami, getting released after Dave Wannstedt took over for Johnson.

If nothing else, Druckenmiller's brief NFL career gave him an opportunity to be around Steve Young and Dan Marino, both of whom were inducted into the Pro Football Hall of Fame's class of 2005.

"It was really great," Druckenmiller said. "The first year I came in I was the new quarterback who they were grooming to take over, so I think Steve was a bit standoffish. I certainly can't say Steve and I didn't get along, but the second year we developed a nice relationship. We had a bunch of laughs at the end.

"Dan was probably a little more like my personality. We grew up in the same atmosphere, both being from Pennsylvania. And our styles were a little more similar."

Although Druckenmiller saw it as a good move for his career to leave San Francisco, he said he missed the coaching staff.

"I have a lot of respect for all the coaches," Druckenmiller said. "It's good to see Jim Mora doing good things with the Falcons. Obviously, [then-quarterbacks coach] Greg Knapp was someone I worked close with. And I have all the respect in the world for Steve Mariucci.

"Unfortunately, things didn't go so well upstairs with the transition. I was chosen as the No. 1 pick, and then I was traded after the transition."

It was clear from the beginning Walsh did not believe Druckenmiller had a future with the 49ers, but Druckenmiller said he holds no grudges.

"That's water under the bridge," Druckenmiller said. "We weren't a fit for each other. It's nothing other than that."

But the one thing that does bother Druckenmiller is that he never got a chance to prove himself in games that mattered.

"Everybody said, 'He can't do it.' I just wish I would've gotten the chance to prove it either way. At least, I wanted the opportunity to fail," Druckenmiller said.

Draft guru Mel Kiper Jr. predicted Druckenmiller would have to end up with a team that was willing to show some patience. Here is what he wrote in his 1997 Draft Report:

"Physically, he's more impressive than Peyton Manning, but he still needs polish and has to gain a better understanding of what it takes to direct a sophisticated pro offense. Druck has a huge upside, but he isn't there yet. How far he goes will depend upon the coaching he receives, as well as the patience the organization shows in giving him the necessary time to develop his skills."

In just his second NFL game, Druckenmiller was forced into the starting lineup after injuries sidelined Young and backup Jeff Brohm.

Druckenmiller completed 10 of 28 passes for 102 yards with one touchdown and three interceptions in a 15-12 victory over the St. Louis Rams. His only career touchdown pass was a memorable one, as receiver J.J. Stokes made a leaping 25-yard catch against tight coverage.

"J.J. ran a double move, it was 3-Jet Dino," Druckenmiller said. "I was basically reading the safety on that play. Terrell [Owens] was in the slot, and he was supposed to run at the safety, but he got jammed at the line of scrimmage. J.J. was a big target, so I put it up there for him to go get. He made a great catch.

"It wasn't exactly a pretty game, but we got the win."

Druckenmiller landed with the Memphis Maniax of the XFL in 2001, ranking as the third-leading passer in the league behind Tommy Maddox and Mike Pawlawski. He was named Offensive Player of the Week after throwing for 412 yards and three touchdowns in a 29-23 victory over Chicago.

There was a lot of good that came out of the XFL for Druckenmiller. The man who dated Julie Cialini, the 1995 Playboy Playmate of the Year, when he was with the 49ers met the woman with whom he would settle down. He and his wife, Shelly, have been married since July 6, 2002. They met as employees of the now-defunct Maniax.

After the XFL, Druckenmiller had one final chance at the NFL. But the Indianapolis Colts released him two weeks before the start of training camp in 2003.

"I had always remained active and in shape, but after the Colts, the reality hit me," Druckenmiller said. "I had to get a real job. Working a regular job isn't as much fun as playing in the NFL, that's for sure."

Druckenmiller lives in a Memphis suburb, where he works as a sales manager for ChoicePoint, a data-brokering firm, in the pre-employment screening department. His territories include Virginia, District of Columbia, Maryland, Delaware, and West Virginia.

The quarterback who is credited with single-handedly elevating Virginia Tech to a national football power figured to have a long and prosperous NFL career. Instead, it consisted of three tumultuous seasons.

"I probably could've done some things differently," Druckenmiller said. "Everybody likes to look back, but I can't say I have a whole bunch of regrets. I wish I had handled some things differently. I wish I would've been more patient."

Where Have You Gone?

RANDY KIRK

There is no more specialized skill in football than being a long snapper. And Randy Kirk was a self-taught man.

Although he had illusions of being a starting linebacker in the NFL, when he had finished his eligibility at San Diego State, Kirk began to get the idea how in demand he would become for the ability to whip the ball backward through his legs.

"The pro scouts started coming around, and I was pretty fast so it created some interest," Kirk said. "They'd say, 'I hear you can long snap.' And I was like, 'So what? I'm a linebacker.' And they'd say, 'Yeah, whatever, let's see you long snap.'

"I saw their reaction to my snaps, and that's when I first started to realize that was what they really wanted."

This unique art kept Kirk in the NFL for 13 seasons. He was a nomad throughout his career. The New York Giants signed him coming out of college, but he never played in the regular season with the club. His travels then took him to San Diego, Phoenix, Washington, Cleveland, Cincinnati and back to Arizona.

In 1996, the 49ers signed him as a free agent.

"The highlight was coming here and playing as a 49er," Kirk said. "I'd played for Bill Bidwell [Cardinals] and for Mike Brown [Bengals], and when I came here, it didn't take too long to figure out why the 49ers were winning.

"Timing-wise for me, it was lucky, because I knew I was at the end of my career, and I was able to absorb how Eddie DeBartolo did things and how he made his employees feel important."

Kirk was born in San Jose and attended high school at Bellarmine Prep, where he was a three-sport standout. He remained in the Bay Area, attending DeAnza Community College in Cupertino before finishing his college career with two seasons at San Diego State.

Although he was an honorable-mention All-Western Athletic Conference linebacker, he probably never would have played a down in the NFL if it weren't for his long-snapping prowess.

"I know what hat I have to wear," Kirk said. "I was competent enough to play linebacker to get us through a game if somebody went down. In my mind I was a starter, but they didn't want to hurt me."

Michael Zagaris photo

RANDY KIRK

Linebacker/long snapper · San Diego State · Ht. 6-2; Wt. 235
Born: December 27, 1964 · 49ers career: 1996-1999.

Career highlights: Earned roster spot as free agent with San Diego Chargers in 1987 · Signed as a free agent with 49ers in 1996 · Played 157 games in 13-year NFL career · Also played for San Diego (1987-1988, 1991), Phoenix/Arizona Cardinals (1989, 1994-1995), Washington Redskins (1990), Cleveland Browns (1991) and Cincinnati Bengals (1992-1993).

If you're having a difficult time remembering Kirk's days with the 49ers, he would consider that a compliment. After all, his acquisition in March 1996 signaled a re-emphasis on the special-teams aspect of the 49ers.

In 1995, the 49ers ranked 22nd in net punting average and tied for 24th in field-goal percentage. The next year with Kirk handling the snapping chores, punter Tommy Thompson's net average was the fourth-best in the league, and kicker Jeff Wilkins made 30 of 34 field-goal attempts, a percentage that ranked fourth as well.

During his first three seasons with the 49ers, during which time Kirk did not miss a game, the 49ers qualified for the playoffs every season. Each time they won their first playoff game before falling short in the next round. Kirk showed his speed in the 1998 NFC Wild-Card playoff game against Green Bay when he hustled down the field to recover a Roell Preston fumble on a punt return. The 49ers were always contending for a title, and all that points back to DeBartolo's ownership, Kirk says.

"With the parity in the league, it takes all the little things to set you apart," Kirk said, "and the little things being that Eddie knew who I was and he cared about who I was and he acknowledged me. We were playing for Eddie, instead of playing in spite of Bidwell or Brown."

Kirk, who obviously admired the way DeBartolo built an organization, is now doing a lot of building of his own.

He came back for three games late in the 1999 season when rookie long-snapper Joe Zelenka went down with an injury. But Kirk had already started preparing for life after football, joining a construction partnership with longtime friend Keith Spain.

"It was fun to put the bags on and learn the nuts and bolts about building," Kirk said. "Then I started doing some projects with my dad. I learned more of the business side of it from my dad."

Today, Kirk and his father, Sherrel, run Kirk Enterprises, which specializes in small projects. The transition after a 12-year career in the NFL has not been as difficult because he is working at something that was instilled in him at an early age.

"I enjoy it," he said. "I've been around it my whole life. My dad was in the business, so when I was a kid they didn't have babysitters to handle my brother and me. They just put a broom or a shovel in our hands and told us to get to work."

Kirk lives in Morgan Hill, south of San Jose, and he still follows the 49ers, but he isn't much into going to games. He had tickets to a "Monday Night Game" in 2003 but it turned into a stress test.

He didn't know where to park, because he always took the team bus to games. People where honking at him, and then he had a difficult time finding his seats, creating more angst from those around him who knew where they were going.

"I ended up leaving just after halftime," he said.

GARY PLUMMER

After losing to the Dallas Cowboys two straight years in the NFC Championship Game, the 49ers were determined to make changes.

Their defense ranked last in the league in yards allowed per rushing attempt, and they needed to do something to slow down their nemesis, Dallas running back Emmitt Smith.

The first action the 49ers took in the 1994 offseason was signing free-agent linebacker Gary Plummer, a Bay Area native who had played his first eight NFL seasons with the San Diego Chargers.

"I don't think anyone mentioned Emmitt Smith by name, but it was specifically told to me that the defense needed to get tougher," Plummer said. "And they thought I was a guy who could help them get there."

The 49ers signed Plummer to a contract on March 24, 1994—two months after Dallas's 38-21 victory over the 49ers in the NFC Championship Game. For nearly another month, Plummer stood as the team's lone free-agent signee.

"Obviously, it was exciting and great that somebody was courting you and telling you that you're the greatest thing since sliced bread," Plummer said. "But after I signed, the reality set in that they were expecting me to make the difference between what they considered success and failure. It was a little intimidating after realizing that.

"That's one of the reasons Kenny Norton and I became such good friends. I was so happy there was somebody else to focus on—not just me."

Norton, signed away from the Cowboys, set off a 49ers' shopping spree of proven defensive players, including Rickey Jackson, Richard Dent, Charles Mann and Toi Cook. Finally, the 49ers attracted cornerback Deion Sanders two games into the regular season.

Plummer, whose style of play prompted comparisons to Jack "Hacksaw" Reynolds and Matt Millen, succeeded in his role of stuffing the run as the team's middle linebacker. Emmitt Smith rushed for 202 yards, averaging 4.3 yards a carry, against the 49ers in the two previous NFC Championship Games. In two games against the 49ers in 1994, Smith was held to 152 yards and a 3.3-yard average.

It was a miraculous journey for Plummer, whose new team destroyed his former team, the Chargers, 49-26 in Super Bowl XXIX that season. It was also the apex of a career for a kid who had to fight to make teams at every level, including high school.

Coincidentally, George Seifert was the man who at once delivered the most crushing blow to Plummer's football hopes and—in the process—motivated him to greatness.

GARY PLUMMER
Linebacker · California · Ht. 6-2; Wt. 245
Born: January 26, 1960 · 49ers career: 1994-1997

Career highlights: Signed with San Diego Chargers in 1986
after three years with Oakland Invaders of USFL · Led
Chargers in tackles three times · Played eight seasons (1986-
1993) with Chargers · Signed with 49ers in 1994 · Tied 49ers
playoff record with 13 tackles in 1994 victory over Chicago
Bears · Started at middle linebacker on 49ers' 1994 Super
Bowl-winning team · Honorable-mention All-NFL in 1995 ·
Played 180 games in 12-year NFL career.

Seifert, then an assistant at Stanford University, was prepared to sign Plummer to a scholarship after watching film of him playing at Ohlone College, a two-year school in Fremont, California.

"He was supposed to give me a scholarship but we'd never met face to face," Plummer said. "When he saw me for the first time, he rolled his eyes."

Just to make sure he had the right guy, Seifert asked incredulously, "You're Gary Plummer?" Then Seifert said the words that would serve as a driving force throughout Plummer's career: "You can't play in the Pac-10."

Said Plummer, "I was six foot, maybe 200 pounds soaking wet with rocks in my pockets, and I had four percent body fat. I was a skinny little kid."

Instead of calling it quits, Plummer took a year off from football, during which time he grew two inches, and concentrated on lifting weights—which had just started to gain popularity—and took great measures to learn the intricacies of the sport.

"It forced me to become a technician and study and learn the game, because I wasn't as big and strong as most guys," he said. "When I finally did grow, I had this advantage most kids didn't have."

He walked-on at the University of California. In another blow to his ego, he was moved to nose guard, because that is where the team was most thin. He prolonged his career when he hooked on as a linebacker with the Oakland Invaders of the USFL, ending his three-year run as the team's leading tackler.

After the USFL folded, he fought his way onto the Chargers. He also volunteered for action on special teams. The final slight of his football career occurred early in the 1994 offseason when the Chargers gave linebacker Junior Seau a contract for $4 million a year.

"We had almost the same statistics, only I had to line up everybody on every play, call the defense and play special teams," Plummer said. "They offered me about 15 percent of what Junior was making."

Vowing never to return to the Chargers, Plummer dove into the free-agent market. Shortly thereafter, he worked out for the 49ers and Seifert.

The previous year, Plummer approached Seifert after the Chargers and 49ers participated in a combined practice during training camp in Rocklin, California.

"I told George, 'I don't hate you any more,'" Plummer said. "He was totally taken aback, like I'd hit him over the head with a sledgehammer. I told him that I was truly appreciative for what he did for me. I told him, 'I saw your face laughing at me every time I didn't want to run a sprint and every time I didn't want to lift another pound or another 10 reps.'

"He shook my hand and said, 'Congratulations on a great career.'"

After watching Plummer work out on the 49ers' practice field in March 1994, Seifert had some other words for him.

"You might not be able to play in the Pac-10, but you can play for the San Francisco 49ers," Seifert told Plummer.

Finally, Plummer was in a situation where he was wanted and appreciated.

"I was definitely courted with the 49ers and it felt great," Plummer said. "And the most impressive part wasn't even the size of the signing bonus [$500,000]. It was the bouquet of flowers four or five feet in diameter welcoming my wife [Leigh-Anna] to the organization."

Plummer played four seasons with the 49ers, ending his career after the loss to the Green Bay Packers in the 1997 NFC Championship Game.

After 15 seasons of professional football, Plummer's body had about all it could handle. He has undergone 18 surgeries, including a hip replacement four years ago. "I can sleep through the night and walk without pain," he said. He said he is trying to stave off various other problems with a fitness routine that has him biking 100 miles a week.

Plummer, who lives in San Diego, began his eighth season in 2005 as the analyst on 49ers radio broadcasts. Plummer was in the Bay Area for a November 2001 broadcast when his youngest son, Garrett, lost an eye in an accident involving a pellet gun.

During that time, receiver Terrell Owens, with whom Plummer had enjoyed a good relationship, gave support to Plummer and his family. On the morning of November 11, with the 49ers preparing to face the New Orleans Saints, Owens told Plummer he was dedicating that game to Garrett.

"He said, 'The first touchdown pass I get is going to Garrett,'" Plummer said. "And he literally broke down and started crying."

Owens caught two touchdown passes in the 49ers' 28-27 victory over the Saints. "T.O. called Garrett in the hospital, and they've been friends ever since," Plummer said.

STEVE YOUNG

Steve Young's Hall of Fame career got a late start with the 49ers. And his career was cut short, just one season after posting career-best passing numbers.

But there is little doubt that Young squeezed a lot of living into his eight seasons as the 49ers' full-time starting quarterback.

"I don't feel gypped," Young said. "I had an awesome career. I would have loved to have 1987 to 1990 as the full-time starter, but I had come from Tampa Bay and I didn't want to go back to a situation like that. I found a home."

There is no denying Young's brilliance. On August 7, 2005, he was scheduled to be inducted into the Pro Football Hall of Fame in his first year of eligibility.

On June 12, 2000, Young announced his retirement in a press conference held in the 49ers' locker room at their training complex in Santa Clara.

Everybody assumed Young was calling it quits because of an alarming history of concussions. He had sustained at least five from the middle of the 1996 season to early in 1999. That day Young said the concussions played a role in his decision "but it was not the overwhelming factor."

Young can say now what he could not say then. Young said he retired because the 49ers had made the decision to go through a rebuilding process. The club was no longer going to employ a win-at-all-costs attitude.

"A lot of the reason I retired was because it was made clear to me that we weren't going to do that any more," Young said. "They told me they were going to reconfigure things. I was at a place where if we weren't going to have that Super-Bowl-or-bust mentality, it would've been hard to accept."

The media and public assumed he was stepping away from the game as a means of self-preservation, but Young says the situation was not as dire as portrayed. Young said he experienced only a couple days of haziness after sustaining his "career-ending" concussion in a Monday night game September 27, 1999, against the Arizona Cardinals. After that, he said he experienced "zero" symptoms in the years since.

"People didn't trust my judgment," Young said. "I tried to say I was fine, but it just became too big of a story. I had to deal with it in terms of how people perceived it, rather than what it actually was.

"[But] if I had not been ready to retire, I wouldn't have."

Brad Mangin photo

STEVE YOUNG

Quarterback · Brigham Young · Ht. 6-2; Wt. 200
Born: October 11, 1961 · 49ers career: 1987-1999

Career highlights: Inducted into Pro Football Hall of Fame in
2005 · Began NFL career as top selection in NFL
Supplemental Draft in 1984 by the Tampa Bay Buccaneers ·
First-round pick of Los Angeles Express of the United States
Football League · Traded from Tampa Bay to 49ers in 1987 ·
Became 49ers' starting quarterback in 1991 · Made Pro Bowl
seven times · NFL Player of the Year in 1992 and 1994 · Len
Eshmont Award winner in 1992 and 1994 · Super Bowl MVP
after throwing six TD passes in 49-26 victory over San Diego
Chargers in Super Bowl XXIX · All-time NFL
career passer rating leader at 96.8.

Young talked with Denver Broncos coach Mike Shanahan before ultimately deciding to walk away from the game. Young said he did not want to move on to another team and start over at that stage in his career.

Young, who married his wife, Barbara, in 2000, has two young boys, Braedon and Jackson. He continues to run his non-profit organization Forever Young, while being one of four partners in the Sorenson Capital, which provides buyout and growth equity investments.

He also works weekends on the ESPN studio show, *Sunday NFL Countdown*. Despite all of his commitments, he said he is determined to pass the bar exam. Young received his law degree from Brigham Young University in 1994.

Young also passed his biggest test in football that same year, engineering the 49ers' blowout victory over the San Diego Chargers in Super Bowl XXIX.

He has the one Super Bowl title to his credit, but he collected three rings during his 13 seasons with the 49ers. The other two provided invaluable experience in preparing him for his one shot on football's biggest stage, he said.

It took a while for fickle 49ers fans to fully accept Young as the heir to Joe Montana's throne. His tenure with the 49ers was defined mostly for what he had not accomplished—or who he was not—until he broke through with the game of his life in the Super Bowl.

Young's argument for the Hall of Fame became much more convincing after throwing a Super Bowl-record six touchdown passes in a 49-26 victory over the San Diego Chargers in Super Bowl XXIX.

"He had to get a Super Bowl in there somewhere," Bill Walsh said. "He was just a great football player, and that demonstrated it. He had already won MVPs and passing crowns, but the Super Bowl was really his crowning achievement."

But as Young reflects on the accomplishments of the 1994 season, the first thing that jumps into his mind is the victory over the Dallas Cowboys in the NFC Championship Game.

The Cowboys had defeated the 49ers in the playoffs the previous two seasons, so leading the 49ers over that hurdle in the NFC Championship Game was cause for Young to break into a victory lap around muddy Candlestick Park.

"The funny thing is, I was so relieved after winning the championship game that the Super Bowl did not seem overwhelming at all," Young said. "It was such a big deal to beat the Cowboys, and I never really thought, 'We're the 49ers, we can't lose the Super Bowl' until it was too late."

Young said he was able to draw on his two previous experiences at the Super Bowl. He did not play in the 49ers' last-minute victory over the Cincinnati Bengals in Super Bowl XXIII, and he received mop-up duty in a 55-10 victory over the Denver Broncos the next year.

"I prepared to play, physically, mentally and emotionally," Young said of the 49ers' two previous Super Bowl in which he remained mostly on the sideline as Montana's backup. "I was ready to play in those games. It wasn't too far-fetched to think I could get into those games early."

In his first four seasons behind Montana, Young started 10 games and played significant relief roles in several others. Young ultimately benefited from standing on the sideline and watching Montana's artistry, but he was clearly frustrated with his backup status.

After all, this was a man who became the richest player in the game upon signing with the Los Angeles Express of the United States Football League in 1984. He inked a $40.1 million contract, with $34.5 million of the deal paid over 37 years in an annuity. His final payment of $3.173 million is scheduled for 2027.

Young exercised an option in his contract to get his release from the Express, and he moved on to the Tampa Bay Buccaneers in 1985. The Bucs went 3-16 over the next two seasons with him at quarterback.

When Tampa made it clear it was going to draft quarterback Vinny Testaverde with the No. 1 pick in 1987, Young had become expendable. Walsh swung a trade, sending second- and fourth-round picks, and some of owner Eddie DeBartolo's money, to the Bucs to obtain Young.

Although he was stuck behind Montana, Young continued to think of himself as a starter. He even managed to convince himself in preparation before each game that he would be getting the bulk of the playing time.

"If I hadn't had something to engage my mind, convincing myself that I better prepare and get in the mindset that I was starting, I would've gone nuts," Young said.

His desire to get off the sideline, coupled with Montana's territorial right over the position, led to years of awkwardness. Walsh said he mostly stayed out of the way while a controversy engulfed the Bay Area media. Players in the locker room and fans seemingly lined up to take sides in the raging debate—Joe or Steve?

"Joe didn't want to be threatened by another player," Walsh said. "He was the best, and there was no reason why his job should be challenged. And all Steve needed was an opportunity, and he ended up being a Hall of Fame player."

Said former 49ers receiver Dwight Clark, "That was tough. You had two highly competitive guys. One had a lot of success and one was on the brink of it. Both wanted to play more than anything."

Young said his relationship with Montana was as good as it possibly could have been under the circumstances. He said there was "never a cross word" spoken between the two teammates.

"I was attracted to the ideals and the standard that was set with the 49ers," he said. "I wouldn't have stayed if I didn't embrace it."